Tribute to Henry A. "Hank" Rosso

THIS WORKBOOK SERIES is dedicated to the legacy of Henry A. "Hank" Rosso, noted by many experts as one of the leading figures in the development of organized philanthropic fund raising in the twentieth century. This series of workbooks, ranging from *Developing Your Case for Support* to *Building Your Endowment*, was the last project he undertook before his health failed him. The Indiana University Center on Philanthropy, of which he was a founder, is honored to have been asked to complete this project on Hank's behalf. My colleagues and I dedicate this series to his memory.

I am grateful to my colleague Tim Seiler for agreeing to serve as editor. Tim is director of The Fund Raising School, the national and international training program that Hank started in 1974. It is appropriate that this workbook series be tied directly to concepts and materials taught by The Fund Raising School.

By carefully studying the practitioners and scholars in fund raising who came before him, Hank was able to codify and teach principles and techniques for effective philanthropic fund raising. Scores of practitioners who applied his principles have been successful in diversifying their philanthropic fund raising and donor bases in sustaining their worthy causes. Hank was constantly concerned that those who might most need the information of The Fund Raising School might least be able to access it. He developed special courses for small organizations and edited *Achieving Excellence in Fund Raising* to get information into the hands of practitioners. This workbook series was for Hank another attempt to put the tools of effective philanthropic fund raising into the hands of practitioners who could not get to The Fund Raising School courses.

We hope you find this material useful to you in your work. One of Hank's favorite sayings was, "You can raise a lot more money with organized fund raising than you can with disorganized fund raising." We hope it helps you organize and find success in your fund raising activities. As you carry out your work, remember Hank's definition: "Fund raising is the gentle art of teaching the joy of giving."

Eugene R. Tempel
Executive Director
Indiana University Center on Philanthropy

The Excellence in Fund Raising Workbook Series

EXCELLENCE IN
FUND RAISING

WORKBOOK SERIES

THE FUND RAISING WORKBOOK SERIES began with Hank Rosso and his vision of a set of separate yet interrelated workbooks designed to offer practical, high-quality models for successful fund raising. Each workbook focuses on a single topic and provides narrative material explaining the topic, worksheets, sample materials, and other practical advice. Designed and written for fund raising professionals, nonprofit leaders, and volunteers, the workbooks provide models and strategies for carrying out successful fund raising programs. The texts are based on the accumulated experience and wisdom of veteran fund raising professionals as validated by research, theory, and practice. Each workbook stands alone yet is part of a bigger whole. The workbooks are similar in format and design and use as their primary textual content the curriculum of The Fund Raising School as originally developed and written by Hank Rosso, Joe Mixer, and Lyle Cook. Hank selected or suggested authors for the series and intended to be coeditor of the series. The authors stay true to Hank's philosophy of fund raising, and the series is developed as a form of stewardship to Hank's ideals of ethical fund raising. All authors address how their contributions to the series act in tandem with the other steps in Hank's revolutionary Fund Raising Cycle, as illustrated here. It is the intent of the editor and of the publisher that this will be the premier hands-on workbook series for fund raisers and their volunteers.

Dedicated to
the advancement
of ethical
fund raising

**The
Fund Raising
School**

Timothy L. Seiler

General Series Editor

Director, The Fund Raising School

Indiana University Center on Philanthropy

The Fund Raising Cycle

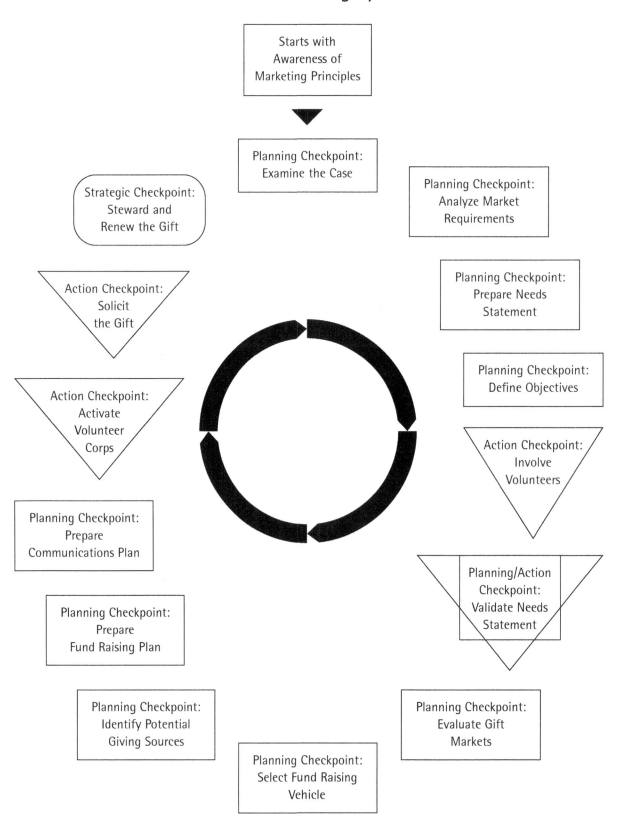

Source: Henry A. Rosso and Associates, *Achieving Excellence in Fund Raising,* p. 10. Copyright © 1991 Jossey-Bass Inc., Publishers. Reprinted by permission of Jossey-Bass Inc., a subsidiary of John Wiley & Sons, Inc.

DEVELOPING
YOUR CASE
FOR SUPPORT

EXCELLENCE IN
FUND RAISING

WORKBOOK SERIES

Series Editor
Timothy L. Seiler

To Emily and Dad

DEVELOPING YOUR CASE FOR SUPPORT

TIMOTHY L. SEILER, CFRE

JOSSEY-BASS
A Wiley Company
San Francisco

Published by Jossey-Bass
A Wiley Imprint
989 Market Street, San Francisco, CA 94103-1741   www.josseybass.com

The materials that appear in this book (except those for which reprint permission must be obtained from the primary sources) may be reproduced for educational/training activities. We do, however, require that the following statement appear on all reproductions:

Developing Your Case for Support, by Timothy L. Seiler.
Copyright © 2001 by John Wiley & Sons, Inc.

This free permission is limited to the reproduction of material for educational/training events. Systematic or large-scale reproduction or distribution (more than one hundred copies per year)—or inclusion of items in publications for sale—may be done only with prior written permission. Also, reproduction on computer disk or by any other electronic means requires prior written permission. Requests to the Publisher for permission should be addressed to the Permissions Department, John Wiley & Sons, Inc., 111 River Street, Hoboken, NJ 07030, 201-748-6011, fax 201-748-6008, or online at http://www.wiley.com/go/permissions.

Readers should be aware that Internet Web sites offered as citations and/or sources for further information may have changed or disappeared between the time this was written and when it is read.

Jossey-Bass books and products are available through most bookstores. To contact Jossey-Bass directly call our Customer Care Department within the U.S. at 800-956-7739, outside the U.S. at 317-572-3986, or fax 317-572-4002.

Jossey-Bass also publishes its books in a variety of electronic formats. Some content that appears in print may not be available in electronic books.

In the resources in Part Four, the following materials from Saint Meinrad Archabbey are reprinted with permission: "Renewing the Heart of Saint Meinrad," the text of the talk at the Regional Benefactors Dinner, the letter sent to insiders, the letter to summer session alumni, the letter to Friends, and the newsletter article with renovation plans.

In the resources in Part Four, the press release announcing a large gift by an individual, the Fellows of Saint Joseph's College March 2000 appeal letter to a donor recognition group, the Fellows of Saint Joseph's College July 1999 letter describing changes in a donor recognition group, and honor roll of donors are reprinted with the permission of Institutional Advancement & Marketing, Saint Joseph's College.

Library of Congress Cataloging-in-Publication Data

Seiler, Timothy L.
  Developing your case for support / Timothy L. Seiler.—1st ed.
    p. cm.—(The Jossey-Bass nonprofit and public
  management series)
  Includes bibliographical references.
    ISBN 0-7879-5245-1 (alk. paper)
    1. Nonprofit organizations—Finance. 2. Fund raising.
  I. Title. II. Series.
  HG4027.65 .S45   2002
  658.15′224—dc21

                                   2001003771

Printing 10 9 8 7 6 5 4 3 2

Contents

Exercises and Worksheets   xiii

Preface   xv

The Author   xix

Part One: Introducing the Case for Support   1

1.   Key Terms   3

The Case and the Cause   3

Case Statement   4

Case Expression   4

Case Resources   5

External and Internal Cases   5

Mission, Goals, and Objectives   5

2.   The Case and the Fund Raising Cycle   7

The Fund Raising Cycle   7

Examine the Case in Step 1   8

Make the Case the Cycle Bedrock   9

Determine Who Develops and Reviews the Case   10

Part Two: Case Components 17

   3. Mission Statement 21

      Examples of Mission Statements 21

      Identifying Organizational Values 24

      Reviewing Your Mission Statement 27

   4. Goals 31

      Examples of Goals 31

      Goals Compared to Mission 31

      Program-Related Goals 32

      Fund Raising Goals 32

      Writing and Reviewing Goals 33

   5. Objectives 37

      Examples of Objectives 37

      Objectives Compared to Goals 38

      Examples of Goals with Objectives 38

      Writing and Reviewing Objectives 39

   6. Programs and Services 43

      Using Stories 43

      Identifying Who Benefits 43

      Collecting Testimonials 44

      Enhancing and Reviewing Program Descriptions 45

   7. Finances 49

      Showing the Costs of Mission Fulfillment 49

      Presenting the Information 50

      Justifying the Need 50

      Examples of Financial Presentations 50

      Preparing and Reviewing Presentations 54

   8. Governance 59

      Selection of Board Members 59

      Board Representation 60

Board Member Strengths 60

Board Functioning and Structure 61

Board Evaluation 62

Information About Members and Advisers 63

Reviewing Governance Information 64

9. Staffing 67

Credentials and Qualifications 67

The Organization Chart 68

Identifying and Reviewing Staffing Information 68

10. Service Delivery 71

Providing Basic Access 71

Offering Superior Service 72

Describing and Reviewing Service Delivery 72

11. Planning and Evaluation 75

Short-Term Fund Raising Plans 75

Long-Term Fund Raising Plans 76

Evaluation 76

Reviewing Fund Raising Plans and Evaluation Processes 77

12. History 81

The Place of History in the Case 81

A Focus on People 81

Writing and Reviewing a History 82

13. Component Checklist 85

Part Three: Putting the Case to Work 89

14. Testing the Completed Case 91

From Internal Case to External Case 91

Case Qualities That Stimulate Donors 93

Matching Case Expressions to Donors 94

Reviewing Your Case Expressions 95

15. Annual Review of the Case   99

Answering Critical Questions Every Year   99

Identifying Why Donors Should Give   102

Conducting an Annual Review   104

16. Moving Forward with the Case   107

Leading the Effort   107

Assembling the Case Resources File   108

Developing and Testing the Case   109

Recognizing All the Case Functions   109

Reviewing and Revalidating the Case   110

Part Four: Resources   113

SAMPLE CASE FILE   115

Our Neighborhood Development Corporation   116

SAMPLE CASE EXPRESSIONS   123

The Case for Renovating the Abbey Church   124

Letter Sent to "Insiders" During Renovation   139

Text of Regional Benefactors Dinner Talk   141

Newsletter Article Detailing Renovation Plans   145

Appeal Letter Sent to Summer Session Alumni   150

Appeal Letter Sent to Friends   151

Brochure Included with Appeal Letters   153

Press Release Announcing a Large Gift by an Individual   157

Appeal Letter to Donor Recognition Group   159

Mailing Describing Changes in Donor Recognition Group   161

Honor Roll of Donors   166

Exercises and Worksheets

Chapter 2

Worksheet 2.1: Examining Case and Cause (Sample)   11

Worksheet 2.2: Examining Case and Cause   12

Worksheet 2.3: Responding to Opportunity   13

Chapter 3

Exercise 3.1: Four-Point Process (Sample)   24

Exercise 3.2: Four-Point Process   25

Worksheet 3.1: Reviewing Your Mission Statement   28

Chapter 4

Exercise 4.1: Writing Goals   33

Worksheet 4.1: Reviewing Goals   35

Chapter 5

Exercise 5.1: Writing Objectives   40

Worksheet 5.1: Reviewing Objectives   41

Chapter 6

Exercise 6.1: Collecting Stories   45

Worksheet 6.1: Reviewing Program and Service Presentations   46

Chapter 7

Exercise 7.1: Gathering Financial Data   54

Worksheet 7.1: Reviewing Financial Presentations   56

Chapter 8

Exercise 8.1: Reviewing Board Characteristics   64

Worksheet 8.1: Reviewing Descriptions of Governance   65

Chapter 9

Exercise 9.1: Identifying Staffing Information   68

Worksheet 9.1: Reviewing Staffing Information   69

Chapter 10

Exercise 10.1: Describing Service Delivery   72

Worksheet 10.1: Reviewing Service Delivery Information   73

Chapter 11

Exercise 11.1: Describing Program Plans   77

Worksheet 11.1: Reviewing Planning and Evaluation   79

Chapter 12

Exercise 12.1: Writing Your History   82

Worksheet 12.1: Reviewing Your History   83

Chapter 13

Worksheet 13.1: Reviewing the Availability of Case Components   87

Chapter 14

Worksheet 14.1: Reviewing Case Expressions for Effectiveness   96

Chapter 15

Exercise 15.1: Identifying Benefits   103

Worksheet 15.1: Conducting an Annual Review   105

Preface

NONPROFITS SEEM TO KNOW INTUITIVELY why they deserve charitable contributions. Making those intuitions concrete and real to the people who will be asked to make gifts to support the work of the nonprofit, however, is a step that requires a methodology and a framework. This workbook provides a methodology for gathering the information essential for developing a case for philanthropic support for nonprofit organizations. It also provides a framework for organizing that information. Finally, it suggests ways to use that information.

In short, this workbook helps you identify and express compelling reasons for people to give you money. Identifying those reasons and developing a case for support is the first step in the complex process that leads to the successful solicitation of charitable gifts.

The development of the case is the foundation upon which the nonprofit organization is built. It is upon this foundation that the organization then seeks philanthropic gift support. If your organization is attempting to conduct an effective development program, a well-developed foundation (case for support) is essential. When the foundation is weak, fund raising suffers. The organization constantly struggles with the effort to come up with materials that excite and inspire volunteers and donors to raise money and give money. When the foundation is strong and solidly built, the information for those materials is understood by all and ready to use. You are always prepared to make the most of fund raising opportunities that will advance your cause.

Audience for This Book

This workbook will be useful for a number of audiences. First, certainly, it offers practical tools and concepts for development staff. It can assist members of the board and particularly of the board's development committee in understanding what is important to the donors they meet with during their fund raising duties. It can ensure that other staff and volunteers involved in fund raising understand the importance of each component in the case for support and how those components are developed. And if you are an executive director of a nonprofit without a development staff, it will be indispensable to you in carrying out your fund raising responsibilities.

Contents

This workbook is divided into four sections, moving from a definition of *case* through a description of the components that make up the case, to a discussion of matching expressions of the case, to the interests of potential funders or donors, and then to a series of resources. Structured exercises in the first three sections assist you in reviewing (if your nonprofit has a history of fund raising) or establishing (if your nonprofit is relatively new) information and data essential to your case. Worksheets guide you in revising and evaluating your materials further.

Part One initially draws a rounded picture of what the case is by defining key terms in case development. Then it discusses what needs to be done in case preparation and who needs to do it. Exercises and worksheets in this section help you examine the basis of your case for support. This section also offers you an overview of how staff, boards, and other volunteers can work together in the development, refinement, and regular review of the case for support.

The chapters in Part Two outline each of the information components used in building a case for support. These components are your case resources. They become the database of information on which you will draw when you formulate case statements and case expressions. Exercises and worksheets in this section allow you to identify and refine such important case resources as your organization's mission, goals, and financial needs.

Part Three addresses bringing all the case resources together in order to take the case for support out to your various publics. This section guides you through a process of testing that your case meets the needs of the constituencies from whom you will seek gift support. It presents some tips for writing effective case statements. It stresses the importance of regularly reviewing and testing the continuing effectiveness of your case for support and of involving key people in this review. Finally, it summarizes the principles of case development and the process of assembling case resources and putting them to work in case statements and case expressions.

Part Four contains a sample of a case resource file and samples of letters, brochures, and other materials that illustrate using the kinds of resources discussed in this workbook to state a case persuasively to potential donors.

How to Use This Book

The most effective way to use this workbook is to go through it step by step, systematically completing the exercises and worksheets and incrementally building a foundation for stating your organization's case for philanthropic support. The savvy user will also revisit earlier sections as she moves toward the conclusion, realizing that later steps will often stir new ideas about the content of earlier steps or ways to improve the execution of those steps.

The ultimate value of this workbook lies in its real and regular use. This is not an exam, a course "blue book." It is not a document to be completed once and then handed in—or worse, one to be completed, read, and put on a shelf. To get long-term value from *Developing Your Case for Support,* you will use it continually—reviewing your case and renewing it over and over. There is dynamic energy in this workbook that will empower your fund raising as long as you make this book a tool in managing this key step in the fund raising process: the development, articulation, and renewal of your organization's case for philanthropic support.

Acknowledgments

This workbook, along with the others in the Excellence in Fund Raising Workbook Series, has been developed from one of the legacies of Henry A. "Hank" Rosso. Hank, with colleagues Lyle C. Cook and Joseph R. Mixer, created the original curriculum for a course on fund raising. A five-day intensive course on the principles of ethical fund raising, it was initially presented in July 1974, in San Francisco. Hank taught the course. He expected perhaps a dozen participants, but his expectations were too low—thirty-three eager learners enrolled in this first-ever offering of "Principles & Techniques of Fund Raising." This pioneer effort marked the beginning of The Fund Raising School, a training program that Hank Rosso and his lifetime partner and spouse, Dottie, conducted for the next fifteen years.

The Fund Raising School moved to Indiana University in 1987, fulfilling Hank's vision that the school would become an integral part of an academic unit within the university. The move was the stimulus for the creation of the Center on Philanthropy at Indiana University in the School of Liberal Arts at Indiana University-Purdue University Indianapolis. The Center on Philanthropy is now the home of The Fund Raising School, and the school is institutionalized in the university, buoyed by academic research that continuously informs and updates its curriculum.

I would like to acknowledge Hank and Dottie for their contributions to the development of The Fund Raising School and for building the school into an internationally recognized training program. I thank them for their lifetime commitment to ethical fund raising and their dedication to training generations of fund raisers how to do correctly the important work of fund raising.

I also thank Hank and Dottie for their gift of The Fund Raising School to Indiana University. I dedicate myself as director of The Fund Raising School to maintaining the dignity and integrity of the school. I see my role primarily as one of stewardship of this magnificent gift, and I commit myself to perpetuating and transmitting the values inherent in ethical philanthropic fund raising.

I would like also to acknowledge the help of several people who made this workbook better than I could have made it alone:

To the reviewers of the manuscript for polishing the text, cleaning up some of my twisted syntax, and making suggestions for organization that helped me clarify the presentation, thank you.

To Johanna Vondeling, "my" editor, for superlative work done with professionalism and kindness, thank you.

To Dorothy Hearst, for your early encouragement and understanding, thank you.

To Queen, for typing and retyping the manuscript, thank you.

To Karen, my wife, for the reminding question, "How much did you write today?" thank you.

To Mark, my son, for the cheer, "Yea, my dad is writing a book!" What a boost! Thank you.

Indianapolis, Indiana   Timothy L. Seiler
June 2001

The Author

TIMOTHY L. SEILER is director of public service and of The Fund Raising School and assistant professor of philanthropic studies at The Center on Philanthropy at Indiana University.

Formerly vice president of Indiana University Foundation, Seiler was a major gifts officer for university development. As director of the foundation's Indianapolis office, he coordinated the constituency development program for the schools and programs of the Indianapolis campus. In an earlier role, he served as development officer for Indiana University Libraries, organizing and managing a comprehensive fund raising program for the library system.

He teaches contract programs as well as core curriculum courses, and he frequently makes conference and seminar presentations. He teaches and lectures on philanthropy and fund raising nationally and internationally.

Seiler has authored and edited numerous fund raising publications and is currently editor in chief of the Excellence in Fund Raising Workbook Series from Jossey-Bass. He is editor of New Directions for Philanthropic Fundraising, a quarterly monograph series addressing the concepts and traditions of philanthropy and their impact on fund raising practice.

Before entering development, Seiler was a teacher and administrator. He is a graduate of Saint Joseph's College in Indiana and has M.A. and Ph.D. degrees in English from Indiana University. He is a member of the Council for Advancement and Support of Education and the Association of Fundraising Professionals (formerly the National Society of Fund Raising Executives) and a former board member and officer of the Indiana Chapter of the Association of Fundraising Professionals.

PART One

Introducing the Case for Support

THE TWO CHAPTERS in Part One of this workbook will help you establish a sustaining context in which you can begin preparing your case for support. Chapter One establishes definitions of key terms. I suggest you read them carefully and note how they are similar to or different from your own definitions. In The Fund Raising School, for example, we define a mission statement a bit differently from the way others define it. Similarly, we make a distinction between a goal and an objective. I believe you will find these and other distinctions helpful as you build your case resources file because you will be able to categorize materials more accurately.

The second chapter in Part One explains the critical role of the case for support in the overall fund raising process. Fund raising involves multiple steps, some of which are undertaken simultaneously. The first step, however, which makes possible all succeeding steps, is the examination of your case for support and the preparation for stating your case for support to those from whom you will seek gifts. This chapter also discusses the importance of leadership in developing the case for support and why it is essential to involve others in the processes presented in this workbook.

Part One contains vital information for anyone involved in fund raising, and I encourage you to read these chapters and complete the exercises and worksheets here before undertaking the tasks in Parts Two and Three of the workbook.

The Case and the Cause

Case Statement

Case Expression

Case Resources

External and Internal Cases

Mission, Goals, and Objectives

CHAPTER 1

Key Terms

THIS CHAPTER DEFINES some key terms that are used throughout the workbook. The discussion of these terms also introduces concepts central to the work of case development. We'll look at the terms *case, cause, case statement, case expression,* and *case resources.* We'll define the *external case* and the *internal case.* And we'll distinguish *mission, goals,* and *objectives.*

The terms *case* and *case statement* are common in fund raising. Although these terms are often used interchangeably, I believe there is a useful differentiation to be made between them, and in this workbook I will follow this differentiation. Here is how I see the difference.

The Case and the Cause

A *case* is the general argument why a charitable organization deserves gift support. The case is bigger than the organization and relates generally to a cause. A *cause* is a set of interests served with dedication; it is a community need that the nonprofit organization is working to meet.

A cause might be eliminating hunger, reducing homelessness, or providing higher education. The case for each nonprofit serving each of these causes is a compilation of carefully prepared reasons why that organization deserves support in serving that particular cause. These reasons may focus, for example, on the organization's present and required resources, its potential for giving greater service to its constituents, the needs it believes it can meet, and its plans for the future.

From this point of view, a case can be seen as an encyclopedic accumulation of information about the organization, its cause, and how it serves its cause.

DEFINITION

Case—the reasons why an organization both needs and merits philanthropic support, usually by outlining the organization's programs, current needs, and plans.

—NSFRE Fund Raising Dictionary

Case Statement

At different times and for different donors, appropriate parts of this case information can be selected and used to present a specific argument why the institution deserves financial support in doing its work now and in the future. A *case statement* is such an argument.

A case statement is not as big as the case. That is, a case statement is a specific illustration of some of the elements making up the full case. Although the case is typically made up of numerous reasons why the organization deserves gift support, not every single reason is necessarily included in each case statement. A case statement focuses on or highlights critical factors important under certain circumstances in arguing for gift support for the organization.

You might liken the relationship between the case and the case statement to the relationship between research gathered for a report and the final report. In compiling information, you include as much material as you can find in support of your topic. In preparing and presenting your report, however, you select only the information that most effectively makes the point you want to make to your chosen audience. You don't use every piece of information. You might then return to your original compilation and select somewhat different information for a different report to a different audience. That is just about the process that obtains in moving from case to case statement. A case statement selects and articulates key points from the overall case.

DEFINITION

Case statement—a presentation that sets forth a case.

—NSFRE Fund Raising Dictionary

Case Expression

A *case expression* is a specific publication or communication (in print or another medium) that contains a case statement. A case expression might be a grant proposal, a brochure, a direct mail letter, an annual report, or any other communication that presents the case for support, and often also directly requests support.

Case Resources

Case resources are the information elements that staff use when putting together presentations for support such as grant proposals, brochures, direct mail letters, and annual reports. In short, case resources constitute the database of all the information and arguments that make up the case and that are then used selectively to develop case statements and case expressions.

Part Two of this workbook helps you gather and refine the most important elements of your nonprofit's case resources.

External and Internal Cases

External case is another term for *case expression,* a presentation of the case in the form of, for example, a brochure, a letter, an annual report, or a speech to a service club, corporation, or foundation that tells the story of the organization and its cause to its constituents.

Internal case is another term for *case resources,* the compilation of information that supports the preparation of the various documents and publications that explain the organization's work.

Mission, Goals, and Objectives

A nonprofit's *mission statement* is a philosophical statement of the core values that guide the organization in addressing a societal need. In developing your case for support, it is essential to distinguish between this statement of organizational values and descriptions of organizational goals and objectives.

A *goal* is a general statement of what an organization intends to do to address a problem or meet a need—that is, how it intends to act on the values expressed in its mission. A mission will often suggest multiple goals.

An *objective* is a specific action or step toward reaching a goal. A goal will often suggest multiple objectives. The first three chapters in Part Two will guide you to formulations of your nonprofit's mission, goals, and objectives that will become an important part of your case resources.

Finally, your nonprofit will function with more focus when it also understands that its *vision* is different from its *mission.*

DEFINITIONS

Mission—what an organization believes in and is today.
Vision—what an organization can become tomorrow.

The Fund Raising Cycle

Examine the Case in Step 1

Make the Case the Cycle Bedrock

Determine Who Develops and Reviews the Case

CHAPTER 2

The Case and the Fund Raising Cycle

FUND RAISING is a disciplined process with many steps. The process is complex, but it is manageable. The multiple steps of fund raising can be viewed as an ongoing cycle, known as the Fund Raising Cycle (see Figure 2.1).

The Fund Raising Cycle

Beginning with the box "Examine the Case for Support" (at twelve o'clock) and proceeding clockwise, there are fourteen steps in the cycle. Each step has a preparation function and has also a strategic action or a planning checkpoint. It is important to note that action is to planning about as one is to three. That is, the fund raising cycle is about three parts planning to one part action. Failure to address the functions in the cycle or acknowledge the checkpoints will end in failure at step 13, the solicitation of the gift. Inadequate attention to any step in the cycle may cause the cycle to break down. It is possible to ask someone for a gift too soon. You will have your best chance for a successful step 13—a prospective giver saying, "Yes, I'll make this gift"—when you pay close attention to each of the twelve steps leading naturally to the asking step.

More generally speaking, Hank Rosso used to say that fund raising is ultimately pretty simple—there are four steps:

1. Plan,

2. Plan,

3. Plan, and

4. ASK!

Asking without planning is likely to result in an answer that you would rather not hear. Asking too soon normally results in no gift or in a gift smaller than is appropriate for the giver's capacity and for the nonprofit's need.

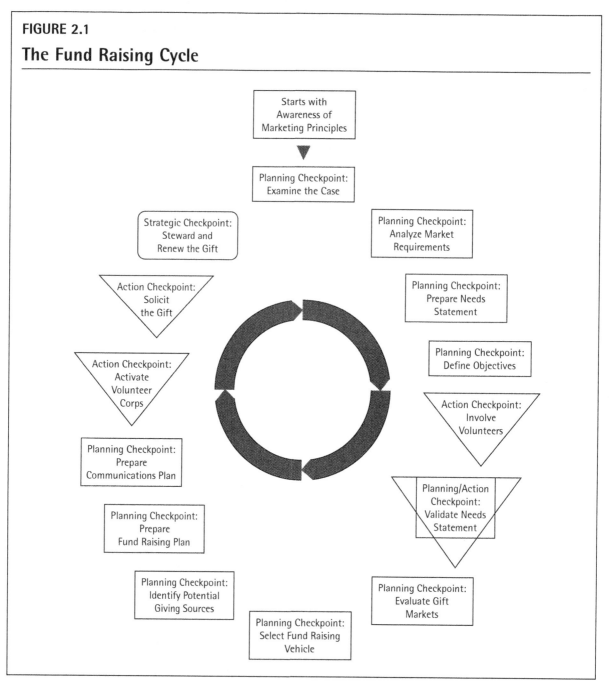

FIGURE 2.1

The Fund Raising Cycle

Starts with
Awareness of
Marketing Principles

Planning Checkpoint:
Examine the Case

Strategic Checkpoint:
Steward and
Renew the Gift

Planning Checkpoint:
Analyze Market
Requirements

Action Checkpoint:
Solicit
the Gift

Planning Checkpoint:
Prepare Needs
Statement

Planning Checkpoint:
Define Objectives

Action Checkpoint:
Activate
Volunteer
Corps

Action Checkpoint:
Involve
Volunteers

Planning Checkpoint:
Prepare
Communications Plan

Planning/Action
Checkpoint:
Validate Needs
Statement

Planning Checkpoint:
Prepare
Fund Raising Plan

Planning Checkpoint:
Identify Potential
Giving Sources

Planning Checkpoint:
Evaluate Gift
Markets

Planning Checkpoint:
Select Fund Raising
Vehicle

Source: Henry A. Rosso, *Achieving Excellence in Fund Raising,* p. 10. Copyright © 1991 Jossey-Bass Inc., Publishers. Reprinted by permission of Jossey-Bass Inc., a subsidiary of John Wiley & Sons, Inc.

Examine the Case in Step 1

The first step in this planning process, and the first step in the Fund Raising Cycle, is to examine your nonprofit's case for support, assembling and evaluating the case resources. This preparation of the case requires an understanding of the principles of marketing. That is, your case for support is not built solely on your financial needs. You do not ask for money just because your nonprofit needs money. Your nonprofit exists in the first place because of a community need. Some real need is not being addressed, and this cause has led to the creation of your nonprofit in the belief that it can meet this need. You are asking for the support that will enable your nonprofit to plan and act for the benefit of the community.

Therefore your general case for support and then your statements of the case and expressions of the case are built on your ability to demonstrate this need and your nonprofit's desire and ability to meet it. The effectiveness of your case with its "market," its persuasiveness in the eyes of potential donors, comes from your service to the cause.

In examining and developing your case for support, then, you want to identify all the reasons anyone should make a charitable contribution to your nonprofit to assist it in its efforts to meet a community need.

Make the Case the Cycle Bedrock

Your fund raising is anchored to your case. After you examine and develop the case in step 1, it supports and shapes every following step. Although you may learn things in each step that enrich your case, the case is your bedrock for each step. It is the lens through which you analyze market requirements in step 2, it identifies needs for your needs statement in step 3 and objectives for step 4, it contains the information—the facts, the stories, and the differences made—that inspires your volunteers to become involved in step 5, and so on throughout the cycle.

Because of its primacy in the fund raising process, your nonprofit's case is deserving of attention and energy. It is not something that development staff write overnight or throw together at the last minute. It is not the brochure included in your direct mail package, nor is it a press release, grant proposal, or campaign folder. These are case expressions (which we will look closely at in Parts Three and Four) but not the whole case. The case is more than any one of these pieces and more than all these pieces together. The case is bigger than any expression of itself.

As you begin the process of examining your case in the remainder of this chapter, you will be considering the relevant, important, and urgent problem that your nonprofit is dedicated to solving, your goals in solving it, your solution for the problem or your improvement on existing conditions, and what you expect to achieve with this solution.

CASE DEVELOPMENT MNEMONIC

Jim Muehling, a course participant at The Fund Raising School, developed this acrostic on the term *case* to summarize the contents of the case:

> **C**ause at hand
> **A**ction addressing cause
> **S**tatement of goals
> **E**xpected results

Use this shorthand list as a tool when developing your case for support.

Worksheet 2.1 illustrates how a nonprofit concerned with protecting the environment might begin to examine its case for support through answering five broad questions. After reading the sample worksheet, use the blank worksheet (Worksheet 2.2) to consider your organization's case for support. Like all the worksheets in this book, this worksheet is a work in progress. Return to it as often as you wish to refine your answers.

Your case for support is built on a cause that exists because of problems and needs in the larger society or in your local community. The value of that case is related directly to your nonprofit's ability to solve problems and its ability to adjust to meet changing market or societal needs. Worksheet 2.3 offers you another way to examine your current understanding of your organization's cause and your organization's abilities for effective action. How prepared are you to draw on case resources in order to make the most of fund raising opportunities?

One of the goals of Part Two of this book is to ensure that your organization has all the most important components of its case in a file, ready to be used throughout the fund raising cycle and whenever special opportunities arise. One of the goals of Part Three is to ensure that this file is regularly reviewed and revised as needed. But before we move on to Part Two, we need to look into who does the work of developing and reviewing the case.

Determine Who Develops and Reviews the Case

Developing the case for support requires leadership from the staff. If you are the executive director of the organization and responsible for fund raising, along with all kinds of other responsibilities, this developmental task falls to you. You are in effect the development director. If there is a separate development director, she leads in developing the case for support.

WORKSHEET 2.1

Examining Case and Cause (Sample)

1. What cause does your nonprofit serve?

My organization is an environmental group concerned with safeguarding our environment: water, air, and proper handling of waste.

My organization serves the cause of a safe, clean, healthy environment.

2. What effect does the work of your nonprofit have?

The community understands the risks of polluting the air and the water through everyday activities as well as through the occasional industrial disaster. People are more aware of how to dispose of trash and waste matter properly, not carelessly.

3. What interests are served by your nonprofit?

We serve the interests of communities who prefer clean, healthy environments for work and for recreation. Families who want healthy environments for themselves and the next generations care about our work. Employers who want to recruit and retain employees by offering the quality of life found in a clean community care about our work.

4. Why is your nonprofit a reason for someone to take action?

We address the problem of air and water pollution and provide ways to clean up the mess.

We develop prevention measures to avoid future problems.

We produce informational packets that teach people how to protect the environment.

5. Why should someone give you money?

We successfully implement programs that remedy current air and water pollution problems.

We provide programs that help prevent future problems by teaching and encouraging people and organizations to practice environmentally safe daily habits.

WORKSHEET 2.2

Examining Case and Cause

1. What cause does your nonprofit serve?

2. What effect does the work of your nonprofit have?

3. What interests are served by your nonprofit?

4. Why is your nonprofit a reason for someone to take action?

5. Why should someone give you money?

WORKSHEET 2.3

Responding to Opportunity

Scenario

You're sitting in your office. A program officer from a local foundation calls you and says she has some extra grant money available. She wants to know how you would use an extra $25,000 if you received it today. She needs your response in the next fifteen minutes.

Your Response

In the space below, write two to three paragraphs making the *case* why your organization deserves this $25,000 grant and describing how the grant will enable your organization to provide benefit to the foundation and to the community.

Hints

- What is the recognized social need your nonprofit addresses?

- What documented evidence about your organization's achievement is available?

- How do you alleviate the need?

Even though the important work of developing the case for support begins with staff, getting others involved is important. Seeking the ideas of key constituents—board members, volunteers, donors, and potential donors—for case development is a particularly effective way to enlist volunteer leadership for fund raising.

In addition, for effective fund raising the case must be clearly understood by all those representing the organization to potential donors. Those seeking support for the case must be able and willing to talk about the case enthusiastically and with conviction to those from whom gift support is sought. Having a role in developing the case for support raises the enthusiasm of volunteers. They learn how to articulate the case for support in their own words. They have a chance to ask questions about those things that puzzle them or to challenge those things that disturb them. This benefits both them and the organization. If they are representative of others from whom you will be seeking gifts, their questions and challenges will tell you where to strengthen your preparation of the case for support.

Figure 2.2 shows the pattern of staff and constituency (including volunteer) involvement in case development. The pattern takes the form of a cycle because case development, like fund raising itself, is an ongoing, iterative process.

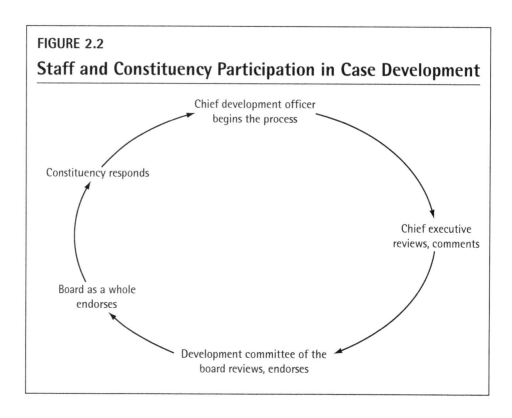

FIGURE 2.2

Staff and Constituency Participation in Case Development

Chief development officer begins the process

Chief executive reviews, comments

Development committee of the board reviews, endorses

Board as a whole endorses

Constituency responds

At each step in the process the case might be revised, refined, or edited. That is, the process through which a number of people participate in case development is not a rubber-stamp review. The collected wisdom of the participants, accumulated step by step, strengthens the case and steels it for its hardest and truest test—the reaction of the constituency that is asked to support the case. The constituency (donors and potential donors) does not write the case or even ultimately approve it; the constituency performs the role of a critical friend by clarifying what donors want and need from the organization. The constituency validates the case.

Similarly, many of the worksheets in Part Two will ask you to identify those who have roles to play in defining, reviewing, and approving individual components of your organization's case, such as mission statements and objectives. Although the case will at times be reviewed in its entirety as just illustrated, individual components may also require individual reviews as they are developed. The ongoing development process will be more efficient and ultimately more successful if you have identified the people who can give you necessary information for defining each component accurately, who can offer insight into meaningfulness and impact, and who have the authority to approve specific kinds of case materials.

Case Components

CASE COMPONENTS, or *resources,* provide information on everything a potential donor might want to know about your nonprofit organization. Your case resources might be already existing documents in your organization's files. If such documents do not currently exist, however, staff will need to create them in order to have all the necessary information for the case available in a written, accessible format. It is the case resources that provide the information on which the case statement is built. Case resources, then, are a database, an information bank, from which specific case statements and expressions are drawn in order to create awareness and interest on the part of potential donors.

A case resources file (or database) consists primarily of information about these organizational components:

- Mission statement
- Goals
- Objectives
- Programs and services
- Finances
- Governance
- Staffing
- Service delivery
- Planning and evaluation
- History

For fund raising purposes, information about all these components must be in the nonprofit organization's office, and that information must be instantly available, accessible, and retrievable. Because case statements and case expressions are developed from the information contained in these resources, the information must also be accurate and current.

The components are listed here from the most difficult but also most important to develop to the easiest and often least important. However, information selected for case expressions tends to follow the inverse order, moving from the easiest yet least important element (to the donor) to the most difficult and most important. That is, brochures, fund raising letters, and other appeals often begin with the history of the nonprofit (it's the easiest thing to write and talk about) and end with the mission statement, if the mission statement is included at all. Why is this?

It happens primarily because nonprofit organizations are often reluctant to write about or speak about the values that inform their work. But this reluctance is a mistake. Successful fund raising depends on matching the values of the donor to the values of the nonprofit. Matching shared values is what successful fund raising is. For that reason the most important component of the case resources file is the mission statement.

What does each of these components of a case resources file consist of, and how is each one important to developing case statements and expressions in the development and management of the fund raising process? Let's take a look at each part of the case resources file to determine its place in building the case for support.

Examples of Mission Statements

Identifying Organizational Values

Reviewing Your Mission Statement

CHAPTER 3

Mission Statement

THE MISSION STATEMENT of a nonprofit organization is a philosophical statement of the human and social needs that it meets. A mission statement explains why the nonprofit exists. It is a declaration of the value or values in which the organization believes and around which it does its work. When it presents the organization's values, a mission statement creates awareness among hearers and readers; it gives them insight.

A mission statement is probably the briefest component of the case resources file, but it is probably also the most difficult and time consuming to prepare and almost certainly the most challenging on which to get people in the organization to agree.

Examples of Mission Statements

A mission statement tells *why* the organization exists, not what it does. What it does is a purpose or program statement. Any statement that contains an infinitive phrase—for example, *to deliver, to serve, to provide*—is a purpose or goal statement, not a mission statement. A mission statement explains *why* the organization does what it does. Let's look at some examples.

An Incorrect Mission Statement

The mission of Concern for Animals is to provide shelter and food for abandoned or unwanted animals.

This statement tells constituents what the organization does—it provides shelter and food for abandoned or unwanted animals. It does not tell why the organization does that. It doesn't tell what value the organization believes in. It doesn't answer the question, Why is it important to do what the organization does?

Presumably the organization provides shelter and food for homeless animals because it believes that animals deserve humane treatment. Why not say that in the mission statement?

A Correct Mission Statement

Concern for Animals believes that all animals have a right to humane treatment. Because we care for all animals, Concern for Animals provides shelter and food for abandoned or unwanted animals.

This mission statement is a straightforward expression of the core value of the organization—the belief in humane treatment for all animals, even abandoned or unwanted ones. In two sentences this mission statement expresses a value, tells what the organization does to fulfill that value, and gives the organization an opportunity to reach out to people who share that value.

FOR-PROFIT EXAMPLES

Even for-profit companies use values-based mission statements to tell customers what the company believes in. Here are two examples:

The Swift Automotive family does business with fairness and honesty. We are committed to creating a friendly, professional atmosphere that exceeds customers' and employees' expectations.

Our palates at the Downtown Restaurant are partial to creative cooking. It is our philosophy that food is not intended solely to satisfy hunger; it must be nurtured and coddled to appeal to all the senses.

Let's examine some more examples.

Incorrect Mission Statements

The Support Life Center is an organization dedicated to providing life-affirming choices to meet the needs of people affected by unplanned pregnancies.

The mission of the Historic Preservation Foundation is to support the Historic Preservation Society, to develop historic sites throughout the state, and to provide opportunities for the people of the state to participate in and contribute to the development and understanding of their state's heritage.

The mission of Global Hope is to combine the resources of individuals and organizations around the world to provide emergency relief and economic and social development.

After reading these statements, do you know and understand the values each of these organizations holds as part of its belief system? You might argue that the values are implicit, that by reading what the organizations do, you can figure out what they believe.

For fund raising purposes, however, it is important to ask if this is sufficient. That is, do you want potential donors to "figure out" what your nonprofit's core values are? Or do you want potential funders to know immediately what your organization believes in and values and to recognize right away when they share values with your organization? Effective mission statements give potential donors a means of identifying the organizations that have beliefs and values that the potential donors share. This is the most important step in turning potential donors into active donors.

Suppose these incorrect mission statements were rewritten.

Correct Mission Statements

Women facing unplanned pregnancies deserve compassion and support. Often, pregnant women do not know where to turn for life-affirming alternatives, assistance, and information. The Support Life Center exists to meet the physical, emotional, and spiritual needs of all who are affected by unplanned pregnancies.

We believe our state's natural history and cultural heritage should be preserved and interpreted to celebrate and educate current and future generations about our past, our present, and our future potential. The Historic Preservation Foundation raises and manages private funds on behalf of the Historic Preservation Society and historic sites throughout the state to supplement state funds for providing and maintaining state-of-the-art facilities, exhibits, and programming that engages visitors of all ages.

Global Hope believes that wherever people are suffering, compassion and hope can help them endure. Global Hope exists to mobilize people and resources to meet the needs of suffering people in a hurting world. This is achieved through a variety of programs including disaster relief and agricultural, educational, medical, and economic assistance.

These rewritten mission statements clearly articulate the core values of each organization. They state clearly the philosophical beliefs that inform the work of the organization. They offer a point of contact, a value through which potential donors who share that value can associate themselves with the nonprofit.

MODELS OF BELIEF STATEMENTS

These eight statements of belief are excellent examples of effective mission statement language:

- We believe that the study of philanthropy should become an enduring field of study in higher education.

- We believe that the study of philanthropy should be interdisciplinary and interprofessional: it should be grounded in the liberal arts and tested by practice.

- We believe that the workshop of ideas is a library, just as the marketplace of ideas is public discourse.

- We believe that students should be encouraged to spend long hours in the library, just as scientists must spend long hours in the laboratory.

- We believe that students should be encouraged to read widely and not be intimidated by the barriers to knowledge erected by specialists called professors.

- We believe that some books are more valuable and enduring than others—there should be a canon—and that it is a matter of continuing debate about which books are most worth reading.

- We believe a good library is a workshop, not a storehouse or an attic. It should be a place to study, to read, to write, and to talk.

- We believe a good library has a lot of books and offers easy access to them.

Source: Robert L. Payton, "An Essay on Donor Intent," presented at the dedication of the Joseph & Matthew Payton Philanthropic Studies Library in the University Library of Indiana University-Purdue University Indianapolis, August 12, 1994. These statements are also engraved on the memorial wall at the entrance to the library. Used with the permission of Robert L. Payton.

Identifying Organizational Values

Exercise 3.1 illustrates a four-point process for developing and writing a mission statement that states clearly the values the organization (in this case a nonprofit called First Step) believes in. Such mission statements reflect the reasons why the organization exists.

Exercise 3.1: Four-Point Process (Sample)

1. Assert the dominant value the nonprofit believes in.

   All persons have the right to self-sufficiency, independence, and self-esteem.

2. Describe the conditions preventing fulfillment of that value.

   Alcohol and drug abuse keeps some persons from fulfilling this value.

3. State briefly what needs to be done to alleviate the conditions described in the second point.

Adequate treatment is necessary to help people recover from alcohol and drug abuse.

4. Affirm that your nonprofit organization challenges the conditions described in the second point and can carry out what is outlined in the third point.

First Step provides treatment for those who abuse alcohol and drugs.

Write a mission statement based on your answers:

All persons have the right to self-sufficiency and self-esteem. Yet today many victims of alcohol and drug abuse are deprived of a sense of self-worth because they cannot pay for adequate treatment for recovery. First Step provides an opportunity for recovery and positive change through affordable, effective counseling and therapy to restore an individual's sense of responsibility and self-worth.

Not all mission statements follow this four-point model, nor do you have to follow the model to write an effective mission statement. However, these steps will help you focus on the values and beliefs of your organization. Use Exercise 3.2 to apply these steps to drafting a new mission statement or revising a current mission statement for your organization. As you complete this exercise, you are providing the leadership for getting the important process of writing an effective mission statement underway.

Exercise 3.2: Four-Point Process

1. Assert the dominant value the nonprofit believes in.

2. Describe the conditions preventing fulfillment of that value.

3. State briefly what needs to be done to alleviate the conditions described in the second point.

4. Affirm that your nonprofit organization challenges the conditions described in the second point and can carry out what is outlined in the third point.

Write a mission statement based on your answers:

Once again, the key idea to remember about your mission statement is that it needs to state boldly and clearly the core values, the fundamental beliefs, of your organization. It needs to become a deeply felt point of contact with donors and potential donors as you and they recognize shared values of importance. Where there is no sharing of values and of core beliefs, there are not likely to be charitable contributions. You need to know the extent of this sharing or lack of it early in the case development process. That's why examining the case for support is the first step in the Fund Raising Cycle—and why developing an effective mission statement is the first element in the preparation of the case for support.

THE ONION TEST

Faculty in The Fund Raising School use what they call the *onion test* to get at the core values of a nonprofit organization. This test peels away the layers from a mission statement, like peeling away the layers of an onion, by asking "Why?" as often as necessary to get to the core value. For example, if a mission statement says the organization exists "to provide . . . ," "to serve . . . ," "to do . . . ," or "to offer . . . ," they ask, "Why?" That is, they ask why the organization does what it does, helping organizational staff peel away each layer to get to the core of the onion, the core value or values of the organization. Frequently, people are surprised at the passion with which they state this core value. When they finally declare the organization does what it does "because we believe everyone deserves fair treatment" (or "a chance at education" or "hot meals"), they are thrilled by the realization that this is a real mission statement, a value they and others believe in and want to support.

Reviewing Your Mission Statement

If potential donors do not believe in the same values that your nonprofit does, they are not likely to be interested in the work that your organization does. Lacking interest, potential donors will not become involved. Involvement precedes giving. Use Worksheet 3.1 to review your current mission statement (use the statement you created in Exercise 3.2 if you have not had a mission statement before or if you think that statement is preferable to your current one).

The purpose of the review is to assist your organization in continuing the process of drafting a compelling mission statement. It should be a statement that will invite the interest and involvement that attract financial support in the form of charitable gifts for your cause. It should also be a statement that reflects the thoughtful input of staff, board members, and key volunteers and that meets the approval of essential staff.

The success of fund raising depends first on a mission that expresses shared values; gift giving is part of mission fulfillment.

Reviewing Your Mission Statement

Mission statement. A philosophical expression of the societal and human problems and needs that an organization addresses. It answers the question, Why does the organization exist?

1. Write your nonprofit's mission statement here:

2. Answer these questions:

   a. Does our mission statement contain an infinitive phrase (*to* followed by a verb)?   Yes ___ No ___

   If you answered yes, the statement is probably a purpose or goal statement and needs to be rewritten.

   b. Does our mission statement state the core values or beliefs that undergird our work? That is, does it answer the question, Why does our organization exist?   Yes ___ No ___

   If you answered no, your statement cannot function as true point of contact with donors and potential donors.

3. Revise your mission statement so it clearly states the philosophy, belief, or value that drives your organization in all its work. Apply the onion test. Ask *why* your organization does what it does until you arrive at core values, beliefs that you hold dear. Write down your revised mission statement here:

4. Answer these questions:

   a. What, if any, additional information do we need to complete this statement?

   b. Who from among the staff, board, and other volunteers should be involved in further development of this mission statement?

   c. Who must ultimately approve and validate our mission statement?

Examples of Goals

Goals Compared to Mission

Program-Related Goals

Fund Raising Goals

Writing and Reviewing Goals

CHAPTER 4

Goals

THE SECOND COMPONENT of the case resources file is a listing of the nonprofit's goals. Goals are general statements identifying what the nonprofit organization wants to accomplish as it seeks to meet the needs or solve the problems described in the mission statement. Goal statements answer the question, What does the nonprofit organization do?

Examples of Goals

Goals are usually stated in ambitious terms not easily measured. Here are some examples of goals:

To help residents achieve health, security, and happiness.

To create public awareness and acceptance of deafness.

To help elementary school youth develop a positive self-concept and learn to get along with others.

Goals Compared to Mission

In writing goal statements, think of goals as outcomes, or ends. They are the statements that guide your organization in its program delivery and operations. Goals should develop naturally from your organization's mission statement. As the mission statement articulates the values of your organization, the beliefs that govern your work, so goal statements tell what your organization will do to fulfill those beliefs.

Program-Related Goals

Goals are usually multiple; that is, your nonprofit will likely have a number of goals that guide it in fulfilling its mission. If your nonprofit runs several programs or categories of program, each program or program category probably has its own set of goals. A neighborhood center, for example, might have three major kinds of programs: children's programs, seniors' and adults' programs, and case management programs. And each kind of program might have several goals:

Children's Programs

To provide preschool, kindergarten, and school-age child care

To provide transportation to and from school

To provide recreational and educational resources

Seniors' and Adults' Programs

To offer GED activities for seniors

To organize social and recreational activities

Case Management Programs

To provide family counseling

To offer employment guidance and job placement

To offer confidential HIV testing

Fund Raising Goals

The goals section of your case resources file might also include fund raising goals for acquiring the money to support the programs. Here are some examples of fund-raising goals:

To increase annual fund income

To expand the donor base

To attract new corporate grants

Writing and Reviewing Goals

In developing and writing goal statements, strive for precision and clarity so that potential donors will understand the goals and will have confidence that in the future they can determine whether your organization has reached its goals. Use Exercise 4.1 to write out existing goals or to begin shaping new goals.

Exercise 4.1: Writing Goals

Write out four to six goals that guide your nonprofit organization in achieving its mission.

1.

2.

3.

4.

5.

6.

Use Worksheet 4.1 to review your organization's goals, including those in the previous exercise. As you did in reviewing your mission, you also need to determine whether additional information is needed and who from among the staff, the board, and other volunteers should be involved in the development or review of goals and in approving and validating the goals as part of the organization's case for support. Once you have worked on general organizational goals, work through the individual program goals and fund raising goals as well.

WORKSHEET 4.1

Reviewing Goals

Goals. General statements of ways in which your organization does address or intends to address the needs expressed in its mission statement. Goals tell people what the organization is and will be doing.

1. Answer these questions:

   a. Do our goals follow from our mission statement? Are they understandable to our constituents?

   Yes ___ No ___

   b. Do our goals tell people what we expect to accomplish?   Yes ___ No ___

   If you answered no to these questions, your goal statements cannot give donors and potential donors a clear picture of the societal and human benefits the organization expects to achieve.

2. Revise your goals so they clearly state what the organization does or intends to do. List your revised goals here:

3. Answer these questions:

   a. What, if any, additional information do we need to complete our goal statements?

   b. Who from among the staff, board, and other volunteers should be involved in further development of these goals?

   c. Who must ultimately approve and validate our goals?

Examples of Objectives

Objectives Compared to Goals

Examples of Goals with Objectives

Writing and Reviewing Objectives

5

Objectives

OBJECTIVES DIFFER from goals in specificity of language. Objectives are not as general or as ambitious as goals. They describe precise results. They are specific statements about the ways the organization is going to reach its goals.

OBJECTIVE DEVELOPMENT MNEMONIC

Objectives should be SMART:

Specific
Measurable
Achievable
Results-oriented
Time-determined

Examples of Objectives

Here are some illustrations of useful objectives:

To conduct a half-day program once every quarter addressing a specific aspect of health maintenance and nutrition for all residents.

To conduct a one-day symposium each year during Deaf Awareness Week consisting of lectures and performances for 500 hearing and deaf participants.

To conduct monthly activities in which students take the roles of others in the group to develop understanding of other people's feelings and needs.

Objectives Compared to Goals

Although, generally speaking, objectives and goals both address what an organization does or intends to do, distinguishing between them allows your organization to be clearer about the social and human good it offers and gives it a tool for better program management. Consider this illustration of the distinction between a goal and an objective. A food kitchen in your community might state that its goal is "to eliminate hunger from our community." This is a lofty goal and certainly laudable.

If you are a potential donor to the food kitchen, however, you might ask how you will know when the goal is reached—or even if it ever can be reached. The problem (hunger) might seem so large as to be overwhelming. Its solution (elimination of hunger) might seem unreachable. You might conclude that the solution is so unlikely as to be unrealistic and therefore choose not to give to the food kitchen because it seems like throwing away good money.

But if the food kitchen, in making its case for support, explains how it intends to reach its goal of eliminating hunger, using specific statements of objectives, a solution might seem possible. The food kitchen might state that its objective is "to provide three meals a day, seven days a week, for at least 250 persons." This result of its program can be measured. You, the potential donor, can know if in fact the meals are being served and to how many persons how many times. The ultimate solution might now seem reachable, the goal achievable.

Objectives, then, are quantifiable, measurable steps taken toward reaching a goal.

Examples of Goals with Objectives

To illustrate further how objectives are specific steps toward reaching goals, here are some examples of goals and the objectives that might accompany them:

Program Goal

To instill in youth a recognition of the dangers of drinking alcohol

Program Objectives

We will provide at least three public information seminars at area schools during the next school year.

We will sponsor an essay and video contest as a prevention program in six of the highest "at-risk" elementary schools.

Program Goal

To help victims, families, and friends manage the trauma of being a victim of a drunk driver.

Program Objectives

We will provide monthly help sessions for victims, families, and friends to help them overcome their losses.

We will provide low-interest loans for up to three years to help victims overcome financial setbacks caused by drunk driving accidents.

Fund Raising Goal

To increase annual fund income

Fund Raising Objectives

We will increase annual giving from individuals by 5 percent in each of the next five years.

We will increase corporate giving and corporate sponsorship by 5 percent annually for the next five years.

We will increase foundation giving by 4 percent annually for the next five years.

Fund Raising Goal

To build a permanent endowment

Fund Raising Objectives

We will complete our $1.2 million endowment campaign by the end of the second fiscal year.

We will complete negotiations for at least three planned gifts in each of the next two years.

Writing and Reviewing Objectives

Now complete Exercise 5.1, making sure that the objectives you write support the goals. Ultimately, every program and fund raising goal in your organization should have its own carefully determined set of objectives that can not only help the organization fulfill its goals and thus its mission but also be communicated to donors and potential donors.

Exercise 5.1: Writing Objectives

Using at least two of the goals you wrote for Exercise 4.1, write at least two objectives for each goal.

Goal 1:

Objective 1:

Objective 2:

Goal 2:

Objective 1:

Objective 2:

Now use Worksheet 5.1 to go back and review and revise the objectives in Exercise 5.1, making each objective precise and measurable. Doing so will create confidence not only in current donors but also in potential donors, who will see that your organization knows what it is trying to do and *how it will do it*. Determine whether additional information is needed, who should be involved in the writing and reviewing of objectives, and who has final approval or validation authority for the objectives as part of the case for support. Each year, every objective for every goal should be reviewed as this worksheet outlines, and revised if necessary.

WORKSHEET 5.1

Reviewing Objectives

Objectives. Specific statements, revised at least once a year, of the ways your organization is going to meet its stated goals. Statements of objectives articulate your programs in brief form and are measurable.

1. Answer these questions, following the SMART acronym:

   a. Are our objectives specific (clearly written so constituents understand exactly how we will meet our goals?   Yes ___ No ___

   b. Are our objectives measurable (so we can evaluate and report on our progress)?   Yes ___ No ___

   c. Are our objectives achievable (are we being realistic)?   Yes ___ No ___

   d. Are our objectives results-oriented (are we aiming for outcomes that will make a difference)?
                                                                                              Yes ___ No ___

   e. Are our objectives time-determined (have we set timelines for activities or dates by which we expect to get certain results)?   Yes ___ No ___

   If you answered no to any of these questions, your objectives cannot tell donors and potential donors how your organization realistically expects to meet its goals.

2. Revise your objectives so they clearly state how the organization will achieve its goals. List your revised objectives here:

3. Answer these questions:

   a. What, if any, additional information do we need to complete our statements of our objectives?

   b. Who from among the staff, board, and other volunteers should be involved in further development of these objectives?

   c. Who must ultimately approve and validate our objectives?

Using Stories

Identifying Who Benefits

Collecting Testimonials

Enhancing and Reviewing Program Descriptions

CHAPTER 6

Programs and Services

THE PROGRAMS and services that your organization offers make up the next key component in your case resources file. This part of your case resources file should include detailed descriptions of how the organization carries out its objectives in meeting the goals that fulfill its mission. It is more effective if you describe these activities as services to real people, rather than as abstractions defined in cold numbers. Potential contributors will want to know how the beneficiaries of your services or programs are better off as a result of your work.

Using Stories

This part of your file is a good place to collect stories. Donors respond to stories because stories give names and faces to people. Potential funders are more likely to be responsive to your fund raising when they can recognize their friends or neighbors in your stories. Stories give life and humanity to programs and services. If you are concerned about confidentiality, it is acceptable to use fictional names. Apart from that, the better the story, the more real it is, the more likely potential contributors are to recognize someone they know in the story.

Identifying Who Benefits

Who is benefiting from your organization's work? The more broadly you can reach in identifying who benefits from your programs and services, the more compelling is your story. So think about both direct clients and beneficiaries beyond those clients. In addition to those persons who are directly involved as recipients of your services, who else is better off as a result of your work?

Are the employers in your community better off because of what your nonprofit does? How about parents and grandparents? Perhaps the school systems in your community are stronger or more effective because of your organization's programs and services. Who else has an enhanced life because of the programs and services provided by your nonprofit organization?

Collecting Testimonials

One of the best ways to build this part of your file is to collect examples of positive things others say about your organization. Have you ever noticed in, say, an automobile service shop letters and notes of gratitude from satisfied customers? Often such notes and letters are posted on a bulletin board in the area where you await the servicing of your own automobile. Many of them are strong testimonials about the value of the work performed by the auto dealer.

Surely you have examples like these of the value of your organization's programs and services. When a client or customer benefits from services you provide and tells you how grateful she is, ask if you have her permission to quote her in some of your materials. If you receive a note or letter praising your programs, ask for permission to reproduce the correspondence in your newsletter or in brochures and other fund raising pieces.

How many times has a local business or government leader cited your organization's work as improving the life of your community? Can you quote these testimonials in your publications?

One of the most effective strategies I've seen is to reproduce such testimonials and send copies to board members, government and business leaders, donors, and potential donors. For example, a local (or even national) newspaper will sometimes carry an editorial praising a nonprofit organization for specific things it does to enhance the lives of its clients or beneficiaries and therefore of the larger community. The nonprofit then copies or reprints the editorial and sends it with a letter from the executive director to key constituents. Such third-party endorsement is an effective way to call attention to your nonprofit's work.

These testimonials from clients, community leaders, and donors validate your organization's case for support by expressing how the organization helps people. Such human interest stories engage the hearts as well as the minds of your constituencies.

Enhancing and Reviewing Program Descriptions

Use Exercise 6.1 to begin collecting materials you can place in your case resources file to make descriptions of programs and services more vivid and compelling.

▸ Exercise 6.1: Collecting Stories

1. Brainstorm about this question: Who benefits from the work (programs and services) of your nonprofit? Write the names or descriptions of the groups here.

2. Focusing on these groups of beneficiaries, think about how you might tell human interest stories about them that will give warmth and flesh and blood to your work. Jot down the highlights of several of these stories.

Use Worksheet 6.1 to review your programs and services and how they are presented. The question about additional information needs special attention here, so you can identify multiple sources of stories, testimonials, and other materials that will make it clear to others how important your organization is in the lives of many people. Program and service descriptions should be reviewed and revised regularly, and fresh materials and information should be sought out.

WORKSHEET 6.1

Reviewing Program and Service Presentations

1. Are the descriptions of your programs and services complete?

2. Are these descriptions concrete and specific?

3. Are these descriptions written in people terms? Is it clear who the beneficiaries are and what impacts the programs and services have on them?

4. What, if any, additional stories, testimonials, or other information do you need to complete these descriptions?

5. Who from among the staff, board, and other volunteers should be involved in further development of these descriptions?

6. Who must ultimately approve and validate program and service descriptions?

Showing the Costs of Mission Fulfillment

Presenting the Information

Justifying the Need

Examples of Financial Presentations

Preparing and Reviewing Presentations

CHAPTER 7

Finances

THE NEXT COMPONENT in the case resources file is the nonprofit's financial information. The financial information links budgeting with objectives and program descriptions. It reinforces the human aspects of your organization's services; that is, the budget numbers themselves are just cold, lifeless figures until donors and potential donors can see how they are connected with services you provide to and for people.

The financial materials in your file should give a clear picture of how the organization both acquires and spends financial resources. This information should clearly establish and validate the need for philanthropic gift support. This is the part of your case resources file that you draw on to justify asking for money, asking for charitable contributions. It draws a financial picture that makes it clear to potential donors why your organization seeks their monetary support.

Showing the Costs of Mission Fulfillment

This is the part of the case for support that lays out clearly and forthrightly the sources of your organization's income. This is where you show potential donors that the government grants, the state or federal funding, the tax appropriation, the United Way allocations, and the like do not, in fact, provide all the funds necessary for conducting the programs and delivering the services that allow the nonprofit to fulfill its mission. The financial picture is where you show as clearly and forcefully as you can the gap between what you receive in income and what it costs in expenses to deliver programs and services. It is the gap between income and expenses that you need to fill with charitable contributions from those donors and funders who share the values expressed in your mission statement and lived through your program and service delivery.

When donors and potential donors understand the finances of nonprofits, they understand the reasons for fund raising.

Presenting the Information

In developing this section of your case resources file, it is good to remember that people learn in different ways. So it's best to present the financial material in at least two ways. You might want to develop a financial report in straight numerical form and in graphic form. Some people will prefer to read a straightforward numerical presentation of the finances: a budget or a balance sheet organized by income and expenditures attributed to programs or to line items. What will have the most impact for others is a graphic representation of the finances in the form of a pie chart or bar graph.

Having presentations of your nonprofit's finances available in more than one format will also be helpful when you are developing various case expressions for multiple audiences for fund raising purposes.

Justifying the Need

Remember that perhaps the most important reason for having an accurate, complete financial picture in your case resources file is that it establishes and justifies your nonprofit's need for philanthropic gift support. As the mission statement justifies your reason for existing, so the financial picture is the raison d'être for fund raising. Fund raising supports mission.

Develop this section of your case resources file carefully and thoughtfully. Have several people in your organization check it and review it. Remember that it needs to be understandable to people outside your organization. Donors, potential donors, and people in the media must be able to comprehend easily the sources of the organization's funding and the ways in which the organization then spends that money on fulfilling its mission.

Examples of Financial Presentations

Here is an example of a snapshot of an organization's finances. They have been condensed into an overview, or financial profile, which gives the reader a quick summary of the nonprofit's finances.

INCOME

Local foundation gift	$19,500
Government grant	11,700
Registration fees	3,380
Special event	5,200
Matching gifts	1,300
Direct mail	3,900
Other grants	6,500
Board contributions	2,600
Miscellaneous gifts	3,900
Interest	780
TOTAL INCOME	$58,760

EXPENSES

Salaries and benefits	$56,278
Training (volunteers)	3,250
In-service workshops (staff)	325
Supplies and materials	6,045
Dues and memberships	598
Travel	1,755
Promotion	3,640
TOTAL EXPENSES	$71,891

Here is another example: a bit more detailed yet still only a financial profile.

INCOME

Contributions	$2,000
United Way	10,900
Criminal Justice Institute	11,000
State grant	12,000
Federal grant 1	42,170
Federal grant 2	101,250
Program grant	45,178
Membership	12,500
Conference registration	12,000
Promotional inventory	500
Interest income	300
TOTAL INCOME	$249,798

EXPENSES

Executive director	$ 33,650
Development director	16,000
Project coordinator	17,800
Membership coordinator	5,800
Office manager	4,800
Case management consultant	1,000
State plan consultant	700
FICA	6,200
Health insurance	6,400
Insurance (liability, workcomp, D & O)	1,500
Contract audit fees	1,500
Accounting fees	8,000
Telephone	6,500
Postage	4,100
Office rent	10,000
Printing	13,000
Office supplies	2,400
Educational materials and resources	9,600
Educational and regional training	19,500
Fundraising	2,000
Equipment maintenance	1,000
Purchase of publications	500
Newsletter	500
Local meeting	1,000
Annual conference	20,000
Mileage and travel	5,700
Registration fees and staff training	3,000
Staff and volunteer recognition	500
Organization dues	1,500
Board development	1,500
Miscellaneous	1,000
Equipment	7,000
TOTAL EXPENSES	$213,650

Figures 7.1 and 7.2 illustrate graphic snapshots of an organization's income and expenses in the form of pie charts. As general, easily readable overviews of the finances of a nonprofit organization, both the graphics and the brief list are good examples of at-the-ready financial profiles usable for publication. If a local business journal were to ask for a general profile of your organization's finances, for instance, these overviews would be ready-made for that public use.

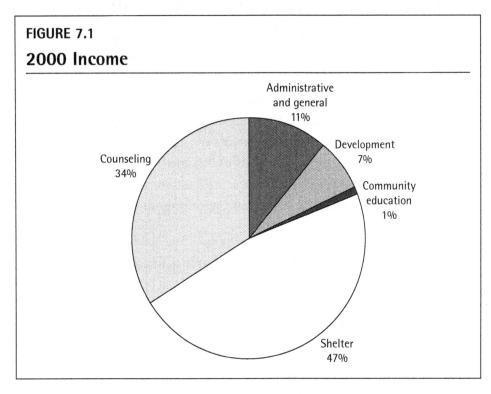

FIGURE 7.1

2000 Income

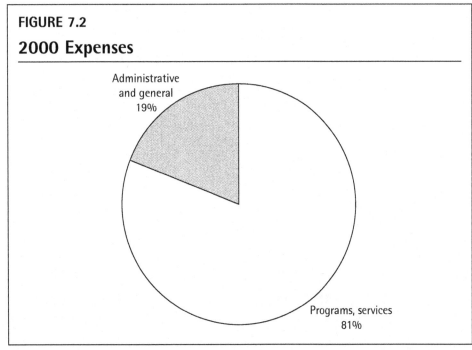

FIGURE 7.2

2000 Expenses

These examples do not, however, contain the level of detail you might want for other purposes, such as budget preparation and review in general or budget preparation for grant proposals or similar fund raising purposes. For more detailed financial accounting and reporting, you will want to gather more detailed financial information.

Preparing and Reviewing Presentations

Exercise 7.1 suggests the level of budget detail that is helpful and instructive to include in the finances component of your case resources file. This kind of budget is helpful internally for reviews of the organization's fiscal health and externally as you make your case for support for fund raising. Complete this exercise to identify your organization's most important expenses and sources of income. Use the blanks provided to identify any additional sources of income (such as fees for service, contracts, and unrestricted gift income) and expenses (such as rental or purchase of facilities, special projects, and your ongoing programs) for your organization.

Exercise 7.1: Gathering Financial Data

Income

Special event	$_____
Matching gifts	$_____
Direct mail	$_____
Grants	$_____
Board contributions	$_____
Miscellaneous gifts	$_____
Interest	$_____
_____	$_____
_____	$_____
_____	$_____
_____	$_____
_____	$_____
Total Income	$_____

Expenses

Salaries and benefits	$_____
Insurance	$_____
Supplies and materials	$_____
Printing	$_____
Dues and memberships	$_____
Rent	$_____
Postage	$_____
Promotion	$_____
_____	$_____
_____	$_____
_____	$_____
_____	$_____
_____	$_____
Total Expenses	$_____

Use Worksheet 7.1 to review the information you gathered in Exercise 7.1 and to develop visuals (such as pie charts and bar graphs) from that material. This review, like the reviews of other case components, should be conducted regularly and materials revised as necessary to present your organization's case as clearly and strongly as possible.

WORKSHEET 7.1

Reviewing Financial Presentations

1. How well does your organization present its budget? Outline the improvements that are needed:

2. If your organization does not already have graphic representations of its budget, create (at least) income and expenses pie charts here:

3. What, if any, additional information do you need to complete your budget presentation?

4. Who from among the staff, board, and other volunteers should be involved in further developing your budget presentation?

5. Who must ultimately approve and validate your budget presentation?

Selection of Board Members

Board Representation

Board Member Strengths

Board Functioning and Structure

Board Evaluation

Information About Members and Advisers

Reviewing Governance Information

CHAPTER 8

Governance

HOW IS YOUR NONPROFIT governed? Who are its trustees or directors charged with holding the organization in public trust? Answers to these questions make up the next element in the case resources file, that of governance. The issue of governance of nonprofits is a key one in attracting charitable support. The governance structure of your nonprofit tells people much about the character and quality of your institution. This part of the case resources file needs to contain the following kinds of information.

Selection of Board Members

How is your governing board selected? Are board members appointed or elected? It is common for nonprofit organizations to have boards that are appointed through a political process. For example, public universities regularly have trustee boards that are in part appointed by the governor of the state. A trustee board of nine members, for example, might have five gubernatorial appointees. The remaining four trustees might be elected by a vote among the alumni. Public library boards regularly have trustees who are appointed by the mayor of the city. Like university boards, library boards typically reserve some seats for another selection process. A library board might have a nominating committee for filling the seats that are not filled by political appointment. In religious organizations it is common practice for board positions to be filled by members of the religious structure. That is, members of the clergy or the ministry hold ex officio board positions. Like universities and libraries, though, religious organizations commonly have the flexibility to bring onto the board additional trustees who are from outside the ranks.

When you are developing the governance element of your case resources file, include an explanation of how your governing board is selected. If there are political appointments, acknowledge that process. If you know what the political appointments try to accommodate—for example, geographical representation, ethnic diversity, some demographic representation—explain that as well. For the board seats that are filled through other means, explain your board's selection process. Is there a nominating committee of the board? If so, who serves on that committee? Describe the process by which the nominating committee suggests names for consideration for election to the board. Explain how new members are elected to the board. Does the nominating committee bring forward to the full board the names of candidates to be voted on? If the full board votes on new candidates, what number or percentage of current board members must vote for a candidate in order for him or her to be successful?

Board Representation

How representative of your nonprofit's service population is your board? If your organization serves youth, are young people on the board? Some nonprofits believe that their client base should be represented on the governing board. That is, they believe that having representatives of the beneficiaries or recipients of services on the board gives the organization an inside look at what the client constituency expects from it. If your board structure reflects this perspective, be sure to include in the case resources file a rationale for this decision-making process in board selection.

Today, perhaps more than in earlier days of nonprofit governance, funders and donors take a close look at how representative the governing board is of the larger community. It is important to remain aware of the changing demographics—in age, ethnicity, and wealth, for example—of your community. Are these variances represented on your governing board?

Foundations in particular today expect to see an appropriate level of diversity on nonprofit governing boards. It is not an exaggeration to say that the "good ol' boy" days are gone. Boards today must reflect the diversity of the community. Remember, moreover, that diversity is not only ethnicity but also gender and age. Diversity should also be thought of as point of view. You would like to have on your nonprofit's board a variety of points of view representing the different perspectives of the community.

Board Member Strengths

Whether your board is an appointed one, one elected by its own members, or a combination of appointed and elected, it should deliberately seek certain strengths in a director or trustee; those strengths become part of the case resources file. Nonprofits recognize that their work, and particularly their fund raising, takes place in a larger context of social, economic, and political interaction. Boards need some connections to this community of social, economic, and political influence. That is why boards are often built by seeking those persons with the greatest wealth, influence, and clout in the community.

Does your nonprofit have a deliberate strategy for board development that enables it to function effectively in this larger context? In other words, your case resources file should describe how your board ensures that it regularly has some directors with the requisite social, economic, and political strengths to position the nonprofit credibly and competitively in the fund raising arena.

Often nonprofits build their boards by strategically seeking specific skills, talents, and expertise that will help the board conduct its work. This is a common practice among nonprofits with limited staff. For example, an organization lacking sufficient staff with accounting or legal expertise will deliberately bring onto the board accountants or attorneys. In a fund raising context, when the chief executive is already stretched thin in overseeing program and service delivery, the organization might bring onto the board someone with experience in organizing and managing special events. At a more sophisticated fund raising level, perhaps the board might recruit someone who could begin a planned giving program for the organization, providing the initial expertise to get the program under way until such time as the organization deems it necessary and affordable to hire staff for this kind of work.

What is your organization's strategy for recruiting to the board relevant strengths and expertise? Be sure to include in the case resources file your plan for bringing onto the board the right kinds of persons with the appropriate skills and talents for effective governance.

Board Functioning and Structure

The governance section of your case resources file should also include a description of how your organization's board functions. For example, is there a committee structure? If so, what are the various committees of the board?

In the earlier part of this chapter, I talked about a nominating committee. A key function of this committee is to think strategically about board composition. Its charge should be to address the representativeness of the board, reflecting as appropriate the nonprofit's constituencies and the larger community, diversity, and relevant skills and expertise.

Many boards have, as well as a nominating committee, a program committee, finance committee, development committee, and executive committee. Your nonprofit might have all these committees and even a few more. If so, describe in the case resources file what each committee does and how it relates to the full board.

Perhaps your nonprofit board has no specific committees but functions as a *committee of the whole*. That is an accepted standard of practice and in fact is a growing trend today. If this is how your board functions, describe the process, and explain how and why this works for your organization.

You have probably heard about one of the banes of nonprofit boards: deadwood. Sadly, nonprofit board members occasionally stop fulfilling their board role but stay around and occupy a seat. There are many reasons why this happens and thus many reasons for deadwood. Sometimes this happens because there is no provision for a timely way of moving people onto and off the board. One way to eliminate deadwood, then, is to set term limits for board members.

It is advisable to have a term limit of two or three years for board service. One common pattern is that a board member is elected or appointed to serve a term of two years. The person is eligible to serve two successive terms—a total of four continuous years of service—but then must relinquish the seat for at least one year. After a one-year hiatus, that board member can come back onto the board for two more two-year terms. And that cycle can be repeated.

Perhaps you seek more continuity. Term limits can be three years, again with the stipulation that two consecutive terms must be followed by a one-year hiatus. Therefore a board member serves two three-year terms, for a total of six continuous years of service. A one-year hiatus in service follows, and then the cycle can begin anew if the person's service will still be of value.

Of course it is advisable to combine the term limit structure with staggered terms. That is, different sets of board members should start (and end) their work in different years so the nonprofit is not always bringing on a totally new board every four or six years.

What is your nonprofit's strategy for terms of office and rules of succession? Describe this policy and associated practices in the case resources file governance section so people know the steps you are taking to maintain a strong board.

Board Evaluation

Another reason that boards occasionally function at less than desirable levels is that they do not monitor their own functions and results. They have no plan or mechanism for evaluating their work and monitoring how well they fulfill their responsibilities as a board. Unfortunately, boards that do not monitor and evaluate themselves become dysfunctional. This is a serious liability for a nonprofit organization and has deleterious effects on fund raising.

Part of the monitoring and evaluating process should be planning for renewal. Boards must find ways to renew their commitment and energy to do their work. An annual retreat is one effective means for renewal. Many nonprofit boards find that getting away once a year from the routine enables them to freshen their perspective and renew their passion for the mission. Additionally, retreats in settings different from the regular setting for board meetings offer board members an opportunity for mingling socially. The social interaction often brings them together in ways that ultimately help them work together more effectively.

Include in this section of your case resources file whatever plans your organization has for monitoring, evaluating, and renewing the board in its work as a governing board. If there are no such plans currently, begin thinking now of how to formulate a plan, involve the key people in developing the plan, and seek approval and adoption of the plan. Taking this step, and implementing a plan for board evaluation and renewal, will position your organization for building confidence in funders that its board is committed to doing its work seriously.

Information About Members and Advisers

The governance section of the case resources file should also house such pertinent information as the complete dossiers of each board member and board organizational material such as bylaws and amendments.

Also included in this section of the case resources file should be information about and descriptions of any special groups that provide advice to the board or the organization itself. Examples are "Friends" groups, advisory councils, visitors groups, and other volunteer groups involved with the board. Such groups are often vitally important for fund raising, particularly in nonprofits whose boards have not been built primarily for functions such as fund raising. It is not unusual for certain types of nonprofit organizations to have boards appointed on a political basis (in the sense of governmental representation). In such instances, board members are often not part of the social and economic power base of the community. They might even believe themselves disenfranchised from the right social and economic circles and therefore disempowered to fund raise. One way to do effective fund raising in such a situation is to form an additional board, one charged with fund raising for the organization. If your organization has such a group in place, be sure to include in this section of the case resources file all the relevant information about how this group is formed, who serves in it, and how the group relates to the formal governing board.

Reviewing Governance Information

The governance component of the case resources file must not be over-looked or taken lightly. The governance characteristics of nonprofit organizations often function as a litmus test for potential contributors. They see the quality and integrity of the governing body as indicators of the strength of the nonprofit cause. Potential contributors have far more confidence in nonprofits with boards that are serious about their commitment to effective governance.

Completing Exercise 8.1 will help you see how your nonprofit's governance looks to outsiders and will suggest areas of improvement that will benefit the organization in general as well as its fund raising.

Exercise 8.1: Reviewing Board Characteristics

1. How representative of your service population is the governing board of your nonprofit? (Be specific.)

2. How representative of your general community is the governing board? (Be specific.)

3. What are the strengths of the current board?

4. What areas of expertise or influence are not currently served on the board?

5. What information, if any, about the board members is not on file in the organization?

6. What can be done to get this information?

7. Who needs to be involved to see that this information is secured?

Next, use Worksheet 8.1 to review the board characteristics you have identified and to contemplate the kinds of changes or additional information that constituents and the community might consider desirable if they are to fund your organization.

WORKSHEET 8.1

Reviewing Descriptions of Governance

1. What documents are currently in place that describe the characteristics identified in Exercise 8.1 and any other important characteristics?

2. Do these documents do a good job of describing the organization's governance to donors, potential donors, and media?

3. What documents need to be added?

4. Who must be involved in drafting, reviewing, or revising these documents?

5. Who has final approval and validation of governance materials?

Credentials and Qualifications

The Organization Chart

Identifying and Reviewing Staffing Information

CHAPTER 9

Staffing

JUST AS THE GOVERNANCE of nonprofit organizations reflects the integrity and quality of the organization, staffing indicates the level of competence and professionalism. Information about the staff of the organization is another vital element in the building of the case resources file.

Credentials and Qualifications

This part of the resources file should contain the credentials and qualifications of the staff. This information in conjunction with staffing patterns shows how the organization delivers its programs and services effectively. Résumés of key staff personnel, both paid and volunteer, should be in the file. Potential contributors will want to know the strengths of the staff who will carry out the work of the nonprofit. What experience do they have, and what kinds of successes have they achieved? Competent, skilled staff combined with dedicated, energetic board members offer a persuasive case for potential contributors to support the organization with charitable contributions.

In addition to having the full résumés of all the administrative and program staff on hand, it is also advisable to develop capsule biographical summaries for staff members for use in grant proposals or in other instances when requests are made for brief information. Such brief summaries might range in length from one or two paragraphs to one page. For example, if your chief financial officer is invited to speak at a conference, the conference coordinators might request a brief biographical summary for use in the promotional materials and printed program. Having such summaries handy and readily retrievable allows you to respond to such requests promptly (and saves you the headache of having to create such biographies under the pressure of limited time).

The Organization Chart

Many organizations still use standard organization charts to illustrate the structure and functioning of the organization's staff. Including the organization chart in this section of the case resources file is one way of showing how the work of the organization is carried out. The organization chart also illustrates the relationship of the staff to the governing board and how the groups interact.

The organization chart may list only positions or job titles. That is, the names of current position-holders do not need to be included. There is certainly nothing wrong with including the names of incumbents should you wish to do so. However, for ease of updating the organization chart and keeping it current, you might choose not to include names, particularly if your organization experiences frequent changes in personnel.

Identifying and Reviewing Staffing Information

In developing your case resources file, do not overlook or shortchange this important element. Staff are the experts in program and service delivery, and their successes (good track records) instill confidence in potential donors and funders that this staff will do the work well and serve the constituencies effectively. So be sure to keep this element of the case resources file current. Have staff review their dossiers at least annually to keep them up-to-date. Encourage staff to include in their updates any continuing education programs and any professional development they participate in to improve their professional competence.

Use Exercise 9.1 to identify your organization's overall staffing design and allocation, including its number of paid staff and volunteers, and to locate or create short descriptions of key positions responsible for management and delivery of services and programs. Include in this section dossiers (résumés, curriculum vitae) of the staff.

Exercise 9.1: Identifying Staffing Information

1. Does your nonprofit have an organization chart or a listing of descriptions of all key positions?

Yes____ No____

2. Does your organization have up-to-date information about the qualifications and credentials of each of the staff who run the programs and deliver the services described in its goals and objectives?

Yes____ No____

3. Who needs to be involved in providing the missing information?

As the information is gathered, begin the process of creating an organization chart (or some other model of the way your organization allocates staff), collecting or updating staff résumés, and writing brief biographical sketches.

4. Where are the organization's files of such information kept?

5. How accessible is this information to the person(s) charged with fund raising responsibility?

Be sure to revise and update this information at least annually, as suggested on Worksheet 9.1.

WORKSHEET 9.1

Reviewing Staffing Information

1. Review the staff dossiers on file. Are they complete and current?   Yes ___ No ___
   Are all key staff accounted for?   Yes ___ No ___

2. If you answered no, what additional information is needed?

3. Who must be involved in completing these files?

4. Who approves and validates these materials?

Providing Basic Access

Offering Superior Service

Describing and Reviewing Service Delivery

CHAPTER 10

Service Delivery

NOW THAT YOU have developed full dossiers and brief biographical summaries for the people who govern your nonprofit and manage its day-to-day work—the governing board and the staff—it's time to describe the facilities and the mechanics of delivery for your programs and services. This component of your case resources file contains descriptions of the physical setting for your programs and services.

Providing Basic Access

Does your organization have a central building where people come to participate in its programs or receive services? Or does it have a larger physical plant with acreage and several buildings? Are there additional service areas, such as off-site centers or "satellite" offices? Does your nonprofit have a traveling program? For example, lending libraries often have bookmobiles that travel throughout neighborhoods, delivering the library to the patrons rather than making patrons go to a library building.

This section of the case resources file needs to provide understandable explanations of how people gain access to your programs and services. As you begin to develop case expressions for fund raising, this information might become especially important for demonstrating the convenience and accessibility of your nonprofit's programs and services. On the one hand, if people can get to your organization's facilities easily or if the organization can take its services to beneficiaries, your nonprofit will be viewed as accessible. On the other hand, it is not uncommon for physical facilities or location or lack of mobility of programs and services to become a liability for nonprofits. Imagine a Meals-on-Wheels program, for instance, that did not have an adequate number of delivery vehicles or had vehicles that were regularly breaking down. Such an organization would not be able to fulfill its mission adequately.

How effective is your organization's physical facility in making your programs and services available? Are your nonprofit's buildings and its service delivery inviting and comfortable?

Offering Superior Service

Occasionally the facilities themselves or the means by which programs and services are made available become distinguishing factors for nonprofits. Those nonprofits that are most visible, most accessible, or most conveniently located have an advantage over those that are difficult to access or from which services are difficult to secure.

What can you say in this section of your case resources file about your nonprofit's facilities or its mechanics of service delivery? What are the distinct advantages of your nonprofit's location? What is superior about its delivery? Are its programs and services portable?

Describing and Reviewing Service Delivery

As you build this section of your case resources file, complete Exercise 10.1 to help yourself think hard about the ways in which service delivery is a distinguishing factor for your nonprofit and how its facilities offer a service advantage to its beneficiaries.

Exercise 10.1: Describing Service Delivery

1. Briefly describe the physical setting(s) in which your organization conducts its programs and services:

2. Describe any mobile delivery of programs and services:

3. If daily or weekly schedules are important, describe those schedules here:

Then use Worksheet 10.1 to review and if necessary revise your materials about service delivery in your organization.

WORKSHEET 10.1

Reviewing Service Delivery Information

1. Do the descriptions in Exercise 10.1 and any other descriptions of service delivery that you have do a good job of showing how accessible your organization's programs and services are?   Yes ____ No ____

2. What additional information do you need?

3. Who must be involved in completing or reviewing these materials?

4. Who approves and validates this information?

Short-Term Fund Raising Plans

Long-Term Fund Raising Plans

Evaluation

Reviewing Fund Raising Plans and Evaluation Processes

CHAPTER 11

Planning and Evaluation

ANOTHER COMPONENT in the case resources file is information about organizational planning and evaluation. Materials here should describe the short-range and the long-range planning processes used by the organization. Program planning should take priority. Because they validate organizational self-assessment, because they document the nonprofit's commitment to carrying out its mission, goals, and objectives, program plans precede fund raising plans. Program plans make clear and validate the nonprofit's understanding that it needs to continue to offer a high level of service in meeting particular community needs. In turn, this continued level of excellence and commitment requires a certain level of ongoing philanthropic gift support. In this way, fund raising plans flow from and follow program plans.

Short-Term Fund Raising Plans

The case resources file should contain the details of the organization's short-range fund raising plans. Think, for example, about the ongoing program support typically generated by contributions to an annual fund. The details will include the dollar goals, the goals for attracting new donors, the plans for encouraging donors to repeat their gifts, and plans for increasing the size of gifts from current donors. In addition, if the organization anticipates that special gift opportunities will supplement the annual fund, this part of the case resources file should describe plans for making these opportunities known to potential donors and for soliciting these gifts.

Long–Term Fund Raising Plans

Beyond the plans for year-to-year solicitation of regular, repeated gifts to support ongoing programs, what are your long-range plans for fund raising? These plans also should be described in your case materials. Again, these plans are driven by program plans. Do program plans mean there will be a future need for capital expansion or improvement? For acquiring land? For building a new facility? For upgrading or expanding technology? Do program plans include expanding human capital? Is there a need for additional staff?

If so, fund raising plans to meet these kinds of long-range needs should address the issue of major gifts fund raising efforts. Perhaps there is even a capital campaign in the organization's future. Then fund raising plans should address what needs to be done to prepare for and manage a capital campaign, the dollar goals for these capital projects, and the ways the organization could pay the fund raising costs for major gifts and capital campaign fund raising.

The long-range plans for the organization might also address the desirability of an endowment. Then a case for support must be built for starting an endowment or expanding an existing one. Fund raising plans will need to address how to do endowment fund raising: Will it require a change in how the organization approaches donors? Will additional staff be required?

Evaluation

Evaluation is an important step in organizational planning. Nonprofits need to have mechanisms in place for checking efficiency and effectiveness. They need to hold themselves accountable. Evaluation answers some critical questions: Do we do what we say we are going to do? Are our programs making a difference for the general good? Evaluation requires organizations to acknowledge that not every program turns out as they expect or want. That does not mean they have failed. Often people learn important lessons from a program that does not produce the results they seek. Evaluation requires organizations to score themselves and acknowledge these lessons and the places where improvements might be necessary.

From a fund raising perspective, evaluation provides a means for an organization to demonstrate its stewardship of philanthropic resources. Evaluation will show whether it has used gifts as it said it would, information important to donors. It is helpful if an evaluation also reports how gifts have made a difference in improving programs and services. Undertaking evaluation also means acknowledging the effectiveness of the organization's fund raising. When evaluation finds a high level of effectiveness, those results can build confidence in donors that their gifts are prudently applied for the good of the cause.

In Chapter Six I described collecting testimonials about programs and services for the case resources file. You might consider using those same testimonials from satisfied stakeholders, donors, and funders as resources in this section of the file. Donors see such third-party endorsements of your good work as effective measures of evaluation.

Reviewing Fund Raising Plans and Evaluation Processes

Having planning and evaluation documents in the case resources file shows that your organization takes its work seriously and holds itself accountable. Donors and funders have confidence in organizations with clear direction and a high degree of responsiveness and responsibility. Exercise 11.1 will help you pull together information about your program plans, a step that is a necessary precursor to reviewing your fund raising plans and uses of evaluation.

Exercise 11.1: Describing Program Plans

1. What were your nonprofit's major accomplishments in programs and services during the past year?

2. What were its major accomplishments during the last three years?

3. What were some of the program and service goals your organization set last year but did not reach?

4. What were some of the goals it set during the last three years but did not reach?

5. Describe briefly why each goal was not achieved, if the goal should or should not still be pursued, and why.

6. What are your organization's major program and service goals for the current year?

7. Describe its progress toward each goal:

8. What are its major goals for the next year?

9. List any goals you wish another department would undertake because they would support your department:

Once you have ascertained your organization's needs by developing your program plans, complete Worksheet 11.1 by reviewing your organizational and fund raising plans in relation to your program plans. Then describe the *process* by which you evaluate (validate and revalidate) your organization as a whole and specific programs and services.

WORKSHEET 11.1

Reviewing Planning and Evaluation

1. What organizational and fund raising plans currently exist in your organization?

2. Do the fund raising plans directly support the program plans, helping donors see that gifts will ultimately support the mission? (Be specific about how this is accomplished.)

3. What needs to be added to your organization's fund raising planning?

4. What evaluation processes and measures does your organization have in place?

5. What processes and measures need to be added?

6. Who must be involved in creating or reviewing fund raising plans?

7. Who must be involved in creating or reviewing evaluation processes?

8. Who approves and validates fund raising plans and documents?

9. Who approves and validates evaluation processes?

The Place of History in the Case

A Focus on People

Writing and Reviewing a History

CHAPTER 12

History

THE FINAL MAJOR COMPONENT of the case resources file is the history of your nonprofit organization. In developing the materials relevant to its history, the organization should avoid the tedious tabulation of data. Instead, in tracing its history a nonprofit should focus on its accomplishments in terms of service to its constituencies and its communities. A history of achievements establishes the past effectiveness of the nonprofit in meeting community needs or solving problems and suggests that it has the ability to reach its goals for the future.

The Place of History in the Case

History is an important validation of the organization's existence, but it is rarely the most compelling motivation for philanthropic gifts. Although it is often difficult to admit, it is generally true that the history of a nonprofit is more relevant and interesting to its staff and other personnel than to donors and prospective donors. As I mentioned earlier, organizational history is often given an important place in case expressions, partly because staff find it interesting and also partly because history is generally safe and easy to talk about. However, in building the case resources file, acknowledge that your nonprofit's history has a place in the case for support but only a place and not the central place. The central place is reserved for the mission.

A Focus on People

In building the history element of the case resources file, focus on the persons and the personalities who have created the human history of your nonprofit organization. A brief description of the founding of the organization and its development over time can show the commitment of the dedicated few who gave birth to an idea, nurtured that idea, and grew it into a sustainable organization that benefits both its immediate clients or constituents and the larger community. Short descriptions of the ways particular people have been associated with the organization lend an aura of credibility to the organization's past and ongoing efforts. Both staff members and board members who have served the organization should people the heroic saga of the organization.

Writing and Reviewing a History

Use Exercise 12.1 to write a brief historical description of your organization, remembering to focus on people.

Exercise 12.1: Writing Your History

1. Jot down (a) the main services and programs with which your organization is associated and (b) the names of the people who are central to the history of your organization: founders, funders, staff, board members, and beneficiaries.

2. Write a brief descriptive history of the founding and growth of your organization; write in terms of people, programs, and services, holding dates and other "dry" information to the necessary minimum.

Then complete Worksheet 12.1 to review the history and ensure that it enriches your case for support.

WORKSHEET 12.1

Reviewing Your History

1. Review the history you wrote in Exercise 12.1 or the historical description you are currently using for case expressions. Does it focus on people, programs, and services?   Yes ___ No ___

2. What materials do you need to add or create to make this history more compelling to donors and potential donors?

3. Who will be involved in the creation or review of historical materials?

4. Who approves and validates historical materials?

CHAPTER 13

Component Checklist

THE TEN ELEMENTS outlined in the previous chapters are the key components of your case resources file. If you build your case resources file by systematically addressing these key elements, you will have an operational case resources file that will give you the support you need to develop effective statements of your case for support and case expressions for fund raising.

This chapter offers a list and a worksheet that you can use as a reference and a checklist to ensure that the most important parts of the case components are properly addressed in your case resources file. They will help you think thoroughly about the kinds of information you need to focus on as you develop and complete your case resources file.

The list summarizes the most important things the case resources file must articulate to make each component a vital part of any case statement.

Worksheet 13.1 is intended to be used as a review of the work that has been done and that remains to be done on key items for your case resources file. It allows you to summarize the items that you have and that remain to be completed and the people responsible for completing or finding them; it also suggests a few additional items, such as letters that confirm the organization's tax-exempt status, that should be included in your file. Use the blanks to include any additional items that you wish to track.

ARTICULATING A CASE TO ATTRACT DONORS

Case Component	Must Articulate
1. Mission statement	An awareness of the cause; insight into the problem addressed by the nonprofit.
2. Goals	The desired achievement that is expected to solve the problem.
3. Objectives	What will be accomplished by reaching the goals.
4. Programs and services	The nonprofit's service to people (including stories of how people benefit).
5. Finances	The expenses of providing programs and services, as a validation of the need for philanthropy.
6. Governance	The character and quality of the organization as shown in its staff and volunteer leadership and governance structure.
7. Staffing	The qualifications and strengths of staff.
8. Service delivery	The advantages, strengths, and effectiveness of the mechanics of program and service delivery.
9. Planning and evaluation	Program and fund raising plans and evaluation processes that demonstrate service commitments, strengths, and impact.
10. History	The heroic saga of founders, staff, and others, and the credibility implied by success over time.

WORKSHEET 13.1

Reviewing the Availability of Case Components

Item	Have	Need	Who Develops or Finds	Date of Completion
Current board list with community and business affiliations	_____	_____	_____	_____
Advisory group list(s) with community and business relationships	_____	_____	_____	_____
Financial statement (balance sheet) for most recently completed fiscal year	_____	_____	_____	_____
Current year operating budget	_____	_____	_____	_____
Biographical sketches of key volunteers and staff	_____	_____	_____	_____
Letters of endorsement and recognition of service	_____	_____	_____	_____
Statistical data that quantify the mission and goals and objectives of the organization	_____	_____	_____	_____
Selected reprints of articles about the organization and its mission	_____	_____	_____	_____
Tax-exempt-status letters	_____	_____	_____	_____
List of major donors, with or without gift amounts	_____	_____	_____	_____
_____	_____	_____	_____	_____
_____	_____	_____	_____	_____
_____	_____	_____	_____	_____
_____	_____	_____	_____	_____
_____	_____	_____	_____	_____

PART Three

Putting the Case to Work

THE FOLLOWING THREE chapters provide tips for testing your case for support for likely success in fund raising.

Chapter Fourteen offers a series of questions that must be answered in order to anticipate the kinds of concerns constituents raise when nonprofits ask them for philanthropic gifts. Going through these questions carefully and making sure that you are provided with the answers will position your organization for success in fund raising. Note that the questions encourage you to think from an external perspective, that of your potential funders and donors. This external perspective helps you develop strong case statements that persuade others to give to your nonprofit.

Chapter Fifteen contains a series of questions that you should review at least once a year. This annual review will help your nonprofit validate and revalidate its case for support. It is vital to hold your case to this kind of scrutiny on a regular basis. This chapter helps you focus on reasons that donors and funders have for making grants and gifts. The exercises here help you think like your donors. Paying attention to this kind of regular review will help you maintain a lively, persuasive, and compelling case for support year after year.

Chapter Sixteen summarizes the key concepts of building a case resources file, developing case statements for general use and for fund raising, and checking the immediacy of your case for support and your case statements. It also reminds you that developing your case for support is an ongoing, cyclical process. The chapter concludes by encouraging you to invest the energy, resources, and time in developing a careful, thorough, well-documented case for support. The work you do up front in building your case for support will pay off in more dollars raised for your nonprofit.

From Internal Case to External Case

Case Qualities That Stimulate Donors

Matching Case Expressions to Donors

Reviewing Your Case Expressions

CHAPTER 14

Testing the Completed Case

THE EXTERNAL STATEMENT of the case for support tells the story of your nonprofit to your constituencies. The real test of your case comes in its expression to various funding sources. Rarely does anyone give a charitable contribution because a nonprofit organization needs funds to balance the budget or get out of debt. The primary reason people give is their belief in the organization and its mission, goals, and achievements. People give to resolve problems for certain groups or to meet larger community needs. Your case externally expressed is what compels people to give to your nonprofit organization.

From Internal Case to External Case

Throughout the previous chapters you have been building an internal case, a database of information and knowledge relating to your organization's case for philanthropic support. The external statement of the case is the ordering and presentation of this information for communications, public relations, and fund raising. The external case expression articulates the cause in the form of documents such as these:

Brochures

Foundation proposals

Direct mail letters

Web site materials

Campaign prospectuses

News releases

Newsletter articles

Speeches

Face-to-face solicitations

Some external case expressions take the form of publications containing general information about the organization that are not intended to raise money directly. Therefore these case expressions do not need to include a fund raising appeal. But for those case expressions developed for fund raising, certain components are necessary.

Preparing case expressions for fund raising is a process of working with the information in the case resources file to develop an internal case which is then refined into the specific expressions of the case. The process translates the information from internal case to external case. All those doing this work—professional staff, board members, and key volunteers—must understand that all the important reasons why the nonprofit organization is valuable and worthwhile must be stated in ways that others understand. All the reasons that seem self-evident to those on the inside must be stated so that those on the outside, the public, can understand why the organization asks for philanthropic support and why it deserves philanthropic support.

THE EXTERNAL CASE

The external case is the case at work.

Source: Henry A. Rosso and Associates, *Achieving Excellence in Fund Raising* (San Francisco: Jossey-Bass, 1991).

In making the transition from developing an internal case document to developing external case expressions, those working on the development of the case should test the case, focusing on answering these questions:

1. What is the problem or social need that is central to our concern (our mission)?

2. What special service or programs do we offer to respond to this need?

3. Why are the problem and our responses to it (programs or services) important?

4. Who makes up the market for our services (who benefits)?

5. Are others doing what we are doing to serve our service market, and perhaps doing it better?

6. Do we have a written plan with a statement of philosophy, objectives, and a program?

7. What are the specific financial needs for which we are seeking private gift support?

8. Is our organization competent (in governance, staffing, and service delivery) to carry out the defined program?

9. Who are the people associated with the organization: staff, key volunteers, and trustees or directors?

10. Who should support the organization? How can these people make gifts, and what are the benefits to them of making a gift?

Case Qualities That Stimulate Donors

In writing case expressions it is helpful to remember that you are trying to stimulate a potential donor to take a series of steps ultimately ending in the decision to make a gift to your organization. Certain qualities must exist in the case expressions to stimulate this sequence of reactions in potential donors. These qualities are excitement, proximity, immediacy, a sense of the future, and meaning.

Case expressions need to excite the reader or listener. Much of philanthropy begins with an individual's emotional response to a nonprofit's need as defined in its case for support. Geographical proximity to the problem arouses emotional awareness. Immediacy is felt when the problem is a real one somewhere in the potential donor's life: when it seems important, even urgent, that the potential donor take prompt action to help solve the problem and when the potential donor learns what happens if he delays in responding to this need. In addition to immediacy, the need to act now, a case expression should offer a sense of the future. The solution to the problem is not a one-time action but an ongoing process. It is unlikely the organization will solve all the problems it sees in the community right now, so what does the future hold in terms of a promise to address the ongoing problems? Finally, what is the meaning to the donor? Case expressions should communicate to the donor the values and benefits of participating that are of importance to him.

Qualities such as these in the expression of the case achieve the desired sequence of beliefs in the donor. Relevance grabs the attention of the donor and focuses her on the importance of the problem or need your nonprofit addresses. A sense of nearness will interest the donor, building a sense of concern on her part. Expression of the immediacy of the problem and of a sense of the future instill in the donor the confidence that your nonprofit has defined the problem accurately and offered a compelling solution. This trust leads to the donor's conviction that your nonprofit will produce the desired results in addressing the problem. Excitement about what can be done will lead to the donor's desire to be part of the program because it will bring satisfaction and enjoyment. Finally, the importance of this project or program will move the donor to take action, to become a participant by making a gift to your nonprofit.

QUALITIES AND RESPONSES

Case Expression Qualities	Sequence of Responses
Relevance	Attention
Proximity	Interest
Sense of the future	Confidence
Immediacy	Conviction
Excitement	Desire
Importance	Action

Matching Case Expressions to Donors

Case expressions are specific documents used in fund raising, and non-profits will typically have multiple case expressions. Your organization probably has several case expressions for its annual fund, for example. It might have a direct mail appeal, grant proposals, and board solicitations. Each of these is a case expression, but the way the case for support is made in each instance will be different. The overall goal of the annual fund is to raise ongoing program support. That need will be expressed one way in a direct mail letter, another way in a solicitation addressed to board members, and yet a third way in a grant proposal.

The direct mail letter, in essence, states a problem, proposes a solution, and requests a gift to implement the solution. This is all done in a largely impersonal way because generally you do not know the recipients of direct mail except by name and address.

In contrast, you do know the members of your organization's board, and normally you will solicit board members in a more personal way. Because they are closer to the organization and more aware of its work, the way you choose to express the organization's need for their ongoing annual support will be qualitatively different from the approach used in imper-sonal direct mail letters.

The case expression is specific to each prospective donor—the recipient of direct mail, the program officer receiving the grant proposal, the board member being asked to make an annual gift. So the expression of the case for support differs in each of these instances, but the case for support itself in general remains the same compilation of reasons why the nonprofit deserves gift support.

Because the case expression always derives from the same case for support but varies for different kinds of donors, the process of creating a case expression is a process of moving from the general to the specific, of assembling all the information about the nonprofit organization in a central location and then employing that information differently for different appeals. Case development, or case preparation, means having a full case resources file to begin the process. The case resources file leads to the preparation of a case expression.

Many organizations have a single document that they call their case statement. However, this document is primarily an internal document. It is usually lengthy, and if you ask the board members and staff about this case statement, they will often say it is pretty dull. They would not want to send it to a potential funder or donor. Nor should they! Such an internal document, whatever its name, should be viewed as a source document for the creation of case expressions used externally.

Reviewing Your Case Expressions

In summary, case expressions are externally focused statements of the case for support. They are specific iterations of the case for support tailored to the audience—direct mail recipients, recipients of grant proposals, board members being solicited, and so on.

At the most general level is the organization's case for support. It contains, either in the form of multiple documents such as budgets, staff dossiers, and fund raising goals or in the form of a single document referred to as an internal case statement, all the information that the organization needs to make its case for support. The case for support, when it is made to the constituencies, is made in different ways. These are external case expressions—specific illustrations of the general case.

Worksheet 14.1 will guide you through a review of your case expressions for effectiveness. Select several publications your nonprofit used in the past year, such as an issue of your newsletter, a general information brochure, a direct mail letter, and a grant proposal. Ask the worksheet questions about each of these publications.

WORKSHEET 14.1

Reviewing Case Expressions for Effectiveness

1. How effectively does this publication make your case for support? That is, does this piece clearly demonstrate how your organization meets a need in the community?

2. How well does this publication position your organization as a problem-solver in meeting the community need?

3. How clearly does it demonstrate that the community benefits from your organization's work?

4. How well does it describe the characteristics that set your nonprofit apart from others doing the same kind of work?

5. If the publication is a fund raising case expression, how well does it state your organization's financial needs (fund raising goals)?

6. How clearly does it instruct readers about how they can make gifts?

7. How persuasively does it convince readers of the benefits they (and others) receive from making gifts?

8. What improvements does your organization need to make in this publication to make it more effective in the future?

Answering Critical Questions Every Year

Identifying Why Donors Should Give

Conducting an Annual Review

Annual Review of the Case

THE KEY TO FUND RAISING effectiveness and success lies in having a fully developed case for support. This case for support prepares your nonprofit organization to articulate clearly, boldly, and readily all the reasons your organization is worthy of philanthropic gift support. These reasons must be reviewed regularly inside the organization and tested regularly outside the organization—in the marketplace where the funders and donors are. The case, that is, must be continually validated and revalidated. Even the best of causes—compelling, urgent, and proximate—must be put to the donor test. Is the cause still relevant and marketable today, every day?

Answering Critical Questions Every Year

It is a valuable exercise for staff to review at least annually some critical questions relevant to building the case for support:

1. Who are we?

2. Why do we exist?

3. What is distinctive about us?

4. What do we want to accomplish?

5. How do we intend to accomplish it?

6. How will we hold ourselves accountable?

These of course are versions of the questions you have used to prepare your case for support and to test your case. They are the questions that challenge the nonprofit to examine its very reasons for existing, and they should always be at the top of staff and board members' minds prior to fund raising attempts. Staff should not assume that last year's fund raising success will inevitably lead to success this year. Staff cannot take it for granted that donors and potential donors know the answers to these questions. It is strategically and tactically important, therefore, that staff and board members quiz themselves regularly on their ability to answer these questions. Even more important, these answers must be communicated to the external constituencies of your nonprofit as well, to those who will provide philanthropic support if they are moved to do so by the answers to these key questions.

At least once a year, your organization's development staff, or the person charged with development responsibilities, should organize and lead a review of these questions. In addition to making sure all staff, board members, and key volunteers know the answers, the review should consider whether donors, and particularly potential donors, are able to answer these questions about your nonprofit. Will their answers match yours? If not, your nonprofit and its donors and potential donors are disconnected. Such a disconnection is not conducive to fund raising on your side and gift giving on the donors' side. What you need to do is connect with your constituencies on the foundation of the case, on the cause your organization exists to serve.

Let's review these questions one more time, concentrating on preparing your organization for fund raising and on donor perceptions.

Who are you? Your organization's name is important, but make sure donors and other constituencies know more than just its name. What work does it do? Why is that work important? Think for a moment of the other nonprofit organizations in your community. How many are there with names like yours? If your organization assists people who have been treated for certain cancers, for example, how many other organizations are there with the word *cancer* in their names? If there is more than one organization in your community with a name like yours, how does your organization stand out from these others?

Never assume that your nonprofit is exempt from this question of identity. Imagine two colleges—I'll call them Warsaw College and Edam College. To students and staff at each college, the schools' differences are clear, but do donors know the difference? Donors hear *college* or *university* and wonder how one is different from another. They might think, to paraphrase the poet, that "a college by any other name would teach as well."

Making your nonprofit's identity clear to donors requires you to have a mission statement that describes the organization's beliefs and values and to maintain your focus on that mission statement—the organization's rationale for existence. What is the problem the organization solves? What is the need it meets? How does it ameliorate that need with its services and programs?

This takes you into the answer to the question, Why do we exist? You must remember and reiterate to others that there is a need for your organization and that is why it exists. This need must be verified by people outside the organization. Whether it's the local news media calling for better schools or extended services for the hungry (or homeless or neglected or abused or the many other needy persons); the local business community demanding a better educated or trained pool of potential employees; or the general population citing quality-of-life needs such as the availability of recreational facilities, cultural attractions, and libraries, others' perceptions of community needs help you explain why your organization exists.

Remember, nonprofits don't exist to provide jobs for their employees or to raise money. Nonprofits exist because the community needs things, and your nonprofit provides one or more of these things. Do not forget this important reality. Remind staff inside your organization and especially remind your constituencies that the organization is there day in and day out, providing necessary services to meet a clearly identified community need.

To get further into separating your organization from similar organizations, ask what is distinctive about your organization. Remember the example of the colleges? If you were to collect the mission statements of any half dozen or so colleges and remove the names from the mission statements, could anyone distinguish one college from another just by reading those missions? Isn't this equally true of the mission statements of other nonprofits? Food kitchens? Environmental groups? Health issue nonprofits? Is it true of your nonprofit?

How does a donor determine that your organization deserves gift support more than another organization with a similar (or perhaps the same!) name does? There's plenty of competition for the philanthropic dollar, so fund raising success is going to depend not only on your organization's mission but on how it describes itself and its work. What is it trying to accomplish? What will it take for the organization to meet the needs for which it exists? The answer to such questions must address programs and services; it must tell donors and potential donors what the organization is doing and perhaps what it has done. Part of your organization's distinctiveness, for example, might be the efficiency and effectiveness with which it achieves what it sets out to do. A good record of previous accomplishments builds confidence that a nonprofit does in fact accomplish what it says it will.

Be forthright and bold in setting out your organization's goals and what it wants to do. Build on previous success. Invite donors to join the nonprofit in thinking big about what can be accomplished today and thinking even bigger about tomorrow. Tell donors what you want to do and how they can help do it.

Also be clear about how the organization plans to accomplish its goals. Set specific and measurable objectives. Think about your plans both short term and long term. Then articulate this planning so donors know where the organization is going and how it's going to get there. Invite them to take this journey with the nonprofit, to join it in accomplishing these noble tasks. Spell out the tactics for carrying out the plans. Show donors how and where they fit in.

Dream big; aim high; go for the solution to the problem; meet the need. And have a plan for measuring, evaluating, and being accountable. Let donors know that the organization holds itself accountable for its plans. Demonstrate the measures for assessing outcomes and impact, and answer the questions donors have about how the community will improve as a result of your organization's work. These steps provide donors with a method of holding you accountable. Demonstrating accountability builds donors' confidence that their gift support will be prudently applied to meeting the need iterated through your organization's mission statement, goals, and objectives and within its programs and services.

Identifying Why Donors Should Give

As I discussed earlier, the first purpose of this review process is to reach agreement internally that the answers accurately articulate the organization's case. The process should involve the board, the staff, and key volunteers. Understanding of and enthusiasm for fund raising and also fund raising leadership will increase as board, staff, and volunteers take ownership of the case and learn how to state the case in their own ways.

The second purpose is to extend the well-developed internal case documentation into external case expressions for the external constituencies. A focus on the potential donor strengthens the case expression. That is, case expressions must identify for potential donors the benefits they and others will receive from the gift they make. You might start by asking, Who benefits? Your organization's case is central to a human, societal need—a cause bigger than your organization—but the organization's programs and services meet this need. So how do the strategies for solving this problem benefit others? And who are the others? Be specific: How do your clients benefit? The neighborhood? The larger community? Society as a whole?

Answering these questions carefully and thoroughly is very important. The more universal the benefits, the broader your nonprofit's appeal—and the broader its constituency for fund raising. Your organization needs to help potential donors see why they should give, and it must offer specific reasons for giving to each distinct funding source.

Use Exercise 15.1 to begin thinking through these donor benefits. Read the benefits given for each major donor group and then add your own donor benefits to the lists.

Exercise 15.1: Identifying Benefits

1. Why should **individuals** give?

   To gain a sense of belonging

   To gain peer recognition

   To build the community

   _____

   _____

   _____

   _____

   _____

2. Why should **corporations** give?

   To improve employee morale

   To be a good citizen

   To receive tax benefits

   _____

   _____

   _____

   _____

3. Why should **foundations** give?

   To support the local community

   To initiate a new program

   To provide "seed" money

   _____

   _____

   _____

   _____

   _____

4. Why should **other funding sources** give?

   _____

   _____

   _____

   _____

   _____

   _____

   _____

Completing this exercise moves you toward a catalogue of answers to the all-important question: What's in it for donors? This is a real, human question, not a rhetorical one. To build your catalogue of answers, write out your own list and then pass this exercise, or one reflecting your organization's specific donor groups, throughout the organization. Ask the executive director for answers. Ask the chief financial officer, program officers, administrative assistants, the receptionist. Ask the board. Then ask other volunteers. Be so bold as to ask some current donors what benefits they think they get in return for their gifts. Be even bolder and ask lapsed donors. You might receive unsettling but also especially enlightening and instructive responses.

Again, what you're trying to assemble here is a long list of what your organization has to offer to donors and the broader community and perhaps ultimately to an improved society. The varied answers should equip you with a number of compelling reasons for donors to give. The quality of this list of reasons is the ultimate test of the persuasiveness of the case for support externally expressed in fund raising communications.

Conducting an Annual Review

Completing Worksheet 15.1 with appropriate staff and board members prior to goal setting and program planning each year will guide you through answering the questions discussed in this chapter. This set of questions can be used for both fund raising planning and evaluation and program planning and evaluation.

WORKSHEET 15.1

Conducting an Annual Review

Ask all key staff and board members and other volunteers to answer these questions:

1. Who are we, and why do we exist? (This revisits our mission. Are we still meeting community needs?)

2. What distinguishes us from others like us?

3. What are we trying to accomplish through our programs and services?

4. What are our plans (goals and objectives) for carrying out our programs and services?

5. What are the evaluation and accountability indicators we use to demonstrate our efficiency and effectiveness?

Leading the Effort

Assembling the Case Resources File

Developing and Testing the Case

Recognizing All the Case Functions

Reviewing and Revalidating the Case

CHAPTER 16

Moving Forward with the Case

NOW THAT YOU have been through the process of building your case resources file and developing case expressions, it's good to review the principles of case development as you prepare to take your case to your constituencies. Preparation and validation of the case for support begins with staff. It is part of the overall organizational planning process and development of data for the management of the organization.

Leading the Effort

If your organization has a development professional on staff, she should be the catalyst and leader in this preparation and validation process. An important reason for this is that the role of the development professional in general often includes serving as an interpreter of the concerns, needs, and perceptions of the external constituencies. An organization's responsiveness to external constituencies has a direct impact on its fund raising capacity.

If your organization does not have a development professional, someone with development responsibilities must take the lead for case development. Ideally, this will be a staff person who not only knows the organization well internally but also has the capacity to interact effectively with external constituencies. This person must be able and willing to bring back inside the organization the perceptions of the external organizations and constituencies where gift support will be sought.

It is not uncommon for development work to uncover that not everything is always perfect among the constituents. The constituents are occasionally misinformed or uninformed (they don't know who you are or why you exist). They may perceive that the organization is not as effective as they would like it to be (they have questions about the practices of its governance and the competence of its staff). Sometimes constituents lack confidence that gifts are needed or that donors' efforts really make a difference (they have no information about ongoing evaluation and accountability processes and the results of those processes).

So development work is sometimes a matter of bringing bad news from the outside into the organization. Staff doing development work must know the organization inside and out and must represent the constituency outside in.

In leading the process of case development, staff gather essential information about the organization and then seek to validate that information and its relevance. They focus on the ten essential case resource components discussed in Part Two:

1. Mission statement
2. Goals
3. Objectives
4. Programs and services
5. Finances
6. Governance
7. Staffing
8. Service delivery
9. Planning and evaluation
10. History

The development person's role is to determine that all these pieces are in place. If anything is lacking, it must be created. The development person will want to have all the information centrally located or at least feel comfortable that he will have cooperation from the various offices and departments with the information so he can have access to it whenever he needs it.

Assembling the Case Resources File

Because this work begins with the development professional but necessarily involves others throughout the organization, the question might arise of the most effective way to go about assembling the case resources file. The exercises and worksheets in Chapters Three through Thirteen are designed to provide a step-by-step process for developing a case resources file and involving all the people who have necessary information or must give approval, and you can and should add steps to these worksheets as necessary to customize them to your organization.

Completing these worksheets and updating them at least annually will help you evaluate your organization's case preparation position. It will give you the opportunity to plan your approach to the task of assembling the case resources file. Finally, it will give you an overview of the others you will need to call on in your organization to help in assembling and validating the case resources file.

Developing and Testing the Case

Case preparation is the first step in effective fund raising. It's the starting point for representing the nonprofit organization to its constituencies. Recall the diagram called the Fund Raising Cycle (Figure 2.1), which illustrates the complexity and intricacy of the fund raising process. As it shows, the first step in fund raising is the examination of your case for support, leading to the development of a case statement. This step is the foundation on which all the external expressions of the case are constructed.

It is worth repeating that case development begins with staff, usually development staff. The development professional provides leadership for organizational planning and for constituency representation. Board members and other staff should also be involved in case development. This results in ownership of the plan (the case), which should in turn result in personal commitment to the case and advocacy of it to others, including prospective donors.

Once the case is developed satisfactorily within the organization, it should be tested among key volunteers, donors, and community leaders. Such testing will ensure that various constituent views are identified and dealt with to strengthen the case. This testing also provides an opportunity to address key concerns and issues that have a potential for negative impact on fund raising. Ultimately, testing the case externally allows the organization to validate that the case is compelling among the markets from which gift funds will be sought or, if that validation is lacking, to reexamine the case, beginning with the mission.

Recognizing All the Case Functions

The preparation of the case itself and of case expressions is the foundation for the seeking of philanthropic gift support as well as for the development of the nonprofit organization. If your organization is attempting to conduct an effective development program, you must have a well-developed case for support! Without a case and effective case expressions, the process of creating the materials necessary to inspire and excite volunteers and donors to raise money and to give money will be a debilitating struggle.

The case and its corresponding expressions enlist donors in ownership of the cause, present a positive image of your nonprofit as a problem-solver, serve as an investment prospectus showing the wisdom of making gifts to your organization, and emphasize your organization's future potential to provide far-reaching benefits.

The case obtains consensus from your organization's major constituencies, members of the board, current donors, prospective donors, and the broader community.

The case is a recruitment tool for enlisting volunteer leadership, including persons beyond the board. It builds confidence in the fund raising effort.

The case tests the markets. It reveals how potential donors feel about your goals. It brings major donors into the planning process and helps them set their own and others' sights for fund raising.

The case is your organization's essential tool for obtaining major gifts. It's that simple. Tailored case expressions are an essential tool for soliciting specific gifts, whether from individuals, corporations, foundations, or other gift sources.

The case forms the basis for additional materials such as news stories, brochures, videos, CD-ROMs, and annual reports.

The case does nothing less than justify your nonprofit's mission and purpose, showing how its programs and services enrich and benefit the community, demonstrating its impact economically, culturally, educationally, spiritually, and aesthetically. Your case proves how your nonprofit profits the community.

If you will spend the time and energy necessary to develop fully your case resources file, involving key persons throughout your constituency in reviewing, critiquing, and endorsing the key components in making your case for support, you will enhance your chances to succeed in fund raising.

Reviewing and Revalidating the Case

It is vital to your ongoing success in fund raising to test your case for support regularly through the external iterations known as case expressions. You need to go forward *with your case in hand* to show contributors why they want to make gifts to your organization.

We in The Fund Raising School recommend that you review and revalidate your organization's case for support at least annually. Examining and testing the case regularly reinforces and revalidates your organization's good work in the community. Your case for support demonstrates that your community profits from your organization's work. As it offers this demonstration of effectiveness, your case for support then attracts the financial resources to fulfill your nonprofit's mission. And all good fund raising comes from mission.

With the strength of your case for support firmly in hand, if you go forth boldly, inviting stakeholders to join in the fulfillment of your mission, you will enjoy many successes in your fund raising.

PART **Four**

Resources

THIS FINAL SECTION of the workbook contains samples for your review and possible modeling.

The sample case file in the first resource is a hypothetical case resources file for a fictitious nonprofit organization. The file is built on the model described in Part Two (Chapters Three to Twelve), and it illustrates how a nonprofit organization might go about the work of bringing together the ten key components of a case for philanthropic support. This sample is descriptive, not prescriptive. It represents one of the ways a nonprofit might begin the process of building its case.

The second resource section presents a variety of external case expressions, including brochures, a newsletter, a speech, and other formats commonly used to communicate general information (as the sample newsletter does, for example) or for fund raising. These examples are from an arch-abbey and a small college in Indiana. (Some illustrations, captions, and other design elements have been omitted owing to space considerations.) Taken together, they are an effective illustration of the various ways non-profits translate their internal case for support into external case statements to ask for charitable contributions to the annual fund, for special projects, and for capital campaigns. As you read through these case expressions, note how the ten components discussed in Part Two appear over and over as the basic building blocks. These examples, too, are for your review and perhaps inspiration as you go about the work of developing your own unique case expressions from your own case resources file.

Sample Case File

Our Neighborhood Development Corporation

Our Neighborhood Development Corporation is a nonprofit organization dedicated to preserving and improving city neighborhoods through housing improvements and neighborhood beautification.

Mission Statement

Stable, thriving communities depend on vibrant neighborhoods. Too often neighborhoods languish and decay in the wake of commercial development. Our Neighborhood Development Corporation believes housing improvements and neighborhood beautification programs can be catalysts for neighborhood revitalization and citizens' sense of belonging to a community.

Goals

To create and maintain affordable housing to build family and neighborhood assets.

To provide leadership in the comprehensive redevelopment and sustainability of a clean, attractive neighborhood.

To develop Neighborhood Watch programs for increased safety and security in the neighborhood.

Objectives

Repair and rehabilitate at least eighteen existing homes in the six downtown neighborhoods in each of the next two fiscal years.

Construct at least twelve new single-family residences in the six neighborhoods by the end of the second fiscal year.

Secure in-kind contributions of trees, shrubbery, and flowers for landscaping each renovated or new home during the next two fiscal years.

Fund or secure funding to replace or add street lights in three of the six neighborhoods in the next two years.

Develop and train neighborhood maintenance crews for every sixteen-block segment in each of the six neighborhoods by the end of the second fiscal year.

Programs

Housing rehabilitation. Our Neighborhood Development Corporation forms partnerships with builders, businesses, and churches to coordinate the rehabilitation of existing houses. Families may do their own work or may secure the help of staff from the corporation.

Housing construction. Our Neighborhood Development Corporation manages the construction of new houses by forming construction groups of paid and volunteer staff. Qualified families must invest their own time in the construction of the house in place of a cash down payment. Each family works with volunteers and paid staff to build its own house and other families' houses.

Landscaping. Our Neighborhood Development Corporation secures in-kind contributions of landscaping materials for the improvement of the neighborhood and individual lots.

Security. Our Neighborhood Development Corporation oversees the formation and management of volunteer Neighborhood Watch programs to create and sustain safe, secure neighborhoods.

Finances

FY 200_

Income

City housing authority grant	$ 23,000
Federal rehabilitation grant	130,000
Home sales	387,000
In-kind contributions	162,000

Charitable contributions: Annual fund

Major gifts (individuals)	$108,900
Corporate grants	55,000
Foundation grants	24,200
Direct mail	9,900
TOTAL INCOME GIFT	$198,000
TOTAL INCOME	$900,000

Expenses

House construction and rehabilitation, landscaping, safety programs	$777,600
Administrative and general	63,900
Fund raising	58,500
TOTAL EXPENSES	$900,000

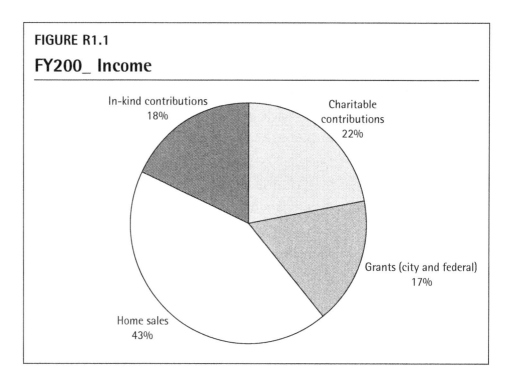

FIGURE R1.1

FY200_ Income

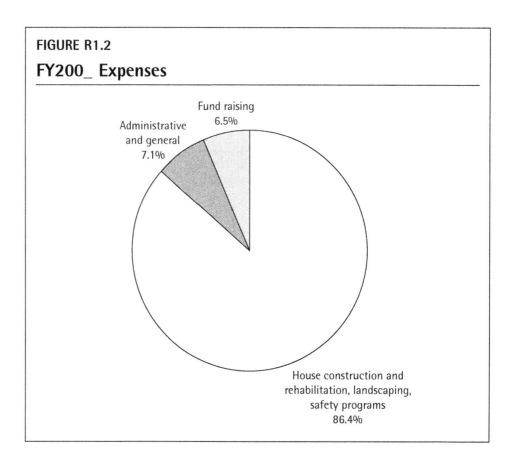

FIGURE R1.2

FY200_ Expenses

Fund Raising Income Projections

[The information in the case resources file on past financial performance might be supplemented by information on fund raising plans, as this following section illustrates.]

Our Neighborhood Development Corporation conducts an annual fund campaign to raise renewable, unrestricted general support. The annual fund consists of major gifts from individuals, corporate grants, foundation grants, and contributions received in response to direct mail.

Given that charitable contributions were 22 percent of this organization's annual income of $900,000 in FY200_, our annual fund income plan is being developed as follows: We assume that total income for the fiscal year will again be $900,000. If charitable contributions equal 22 percent of total income, our annual fund dollar goal will be $198,000. For the sake of this illustration, we will round the figure to $200,000 and use this figure to develop a *gift range chart*. [A gift range chart is a planning tool for determining the most effective way to seek the sizes and numbers of gifts necessary to reach a fund raising goal.] Our gift range chart for raising $200,000 is illustrated here.

TABLE R.1

Our Neighborhood Development Corporation Annual Fund Gift Range Chart FY 200_ Campaign Goal = $200,000

Gift Range	# of Gifts	# of Prospective Donors	$ Per Range	Cumulative $
$10,000	2	10	$ 20,000	$ 20,000
5,000	6	30	30,000	50,000
2,500	16	80	40,000	90,000
1,000	30	120	30,000	120,000
500	60	240	30,000	150,000
250	40	160	10,000	160,000
100	300	900	30,000	190,000
50	200	600	10,000	200,000
TOTAL	654	2,140	$200,000	$200,000

Gift range charts are often based on the premise that 60 percent of the dollar total comes from approximately 10 percent of the donors. In our chart, 60 percent of the dollars, $120,000, comes from about 9 percent of the donors ($n = 54$). This gift range chart is only a beginning point for our planning. We will adjust the dollars per range and the number of gifts in each range as we acquire further information about our constituencies. We might have more money coming from fewer donors or less money coming from more donors. Wise use of this gift range chart will enable us to plan to raise the most money most effectively while we also build a broad base of support.

Governance

Our Neighborhood Development Corporation is governed by a board of directors with expertise in construction and rehabilitation of single-family residences, neighborhood beautification, and neighborhood safety and security. The board also has members with expertise and experience in nonprofit management, volunteer recruitment and motivation, and fund raising.

The board is made up of seventeen members: five are mayoral appointments; twelve are nominated and elected by the board itself.

Members serve two- or three-year terms, renewable once. After two successive terms, members must leave the board for at least one year. After that year they can be reelected.

The board meets six times a year.

The committees of the board are the Executive, Finance and Administration, Nominating, Program, and Development Committees. These committees also have specific subcommittees.

Officers of the board include a president, vice president, secretary, and treasurer.

In addition to the governing board, each committee is served by advisory members who provide specific program expertise.

[A full case resources file also contains a list of board members, information about members' organizational affiliations and titles, and brief descriptions of their qualifications. Ideally the case resources file contains a full résumé for each board member.]

Staffing

The paid staff of Our Neighborhood Development Corporation includes an executive director, four program directors, a chief operating officer, and a director of development.

Each paid staff person has experience and expertise in her or his field of specialty.

In addition to paid staff, many volunteers assist Our Neighborhood Development Corporation in program delivery and fund raising.

[A full case resources file also contains a list of administrative and program staff along with full résumés. The case resources file should also contain résumés for key volunteers who work regularly for the nonprofit organization.]

Service Delivery

Our Neighborhood Development Corporation maintains a central office at 37 East Central Street. The full-time staff are housed in this office. Additionally, the organization uses existing offices or constructs temporary ones for its on-site neighborhood work.

Planning and Evaluation

[This section contains all documents developed in strategic planning. Our Neighborhood Development Corporation includes its strategic plan here along with indicators of progress evaluation measures. It records any changes in plans and provides explanations for the changes. When long-term goals are not met or are changed, a document explains why. The strategic plan and indicators of progress are monitored quarterly and revised annually. The plan includes program goals and objectives and fund raising goals and objectives.]

History

[This part of the case resources file contains pertinent information about the founding and history of Our Neighborhood Development Corporation. Testimonials to the value of the organization's work may be contained in this section, gathered from current and former staff, board members, volunteers, and beneficiaries of the organization's services. Editorials, columns, feature stories, and other endorsements of the organization's work may be filed here for ready reference.]

Sample Case Expressions

Renewing the Heart
of Saint Meinrad

One thing I asked of the Lord,
that will I seek after;
to live in the house of the Lord
all the days of my life,
to behold the beauty of the Lord
and to inquire in his temple.
(Ps. 27:4)

✠   ✠   ✠

This psalm is prayed regularly at the Divine Office for
Sunday Vigils by the monks of Saint Meinrad Archabbey.
In many ways, this verse captures the essence of monastic life.
It also focuses attention on the place where the meaning
of the monastic life is experienced and expressed:
the Archabbey Church.
The church symbolizes the very heart of Saint Meinrad Archabbey.
From it flows the meaning and the motivation
for everything Saint Meinrad is and does.

Saint Meinrad Today

Since its founding in 1854 by the Benedictine Abbey of Maria Einsiedeln in Switzerland, Saint Meinrad has grown steadily. Today, Saint Meinrad is a nationally recognized spiritual and educational center. The Benedictine community, the lifeblood of the institution, continues to attract members to its life of prayer and work. The College and School of Theology offer education and formation to priesthood candidates, religious and Catholic lay leaders. And increasingly, retreatants and other guests come to the "holy hill" seeking spiritual guidance, rest and solitude.

Throughout its history, Saint Meinrad has not wavered in its commitment to meet the needs of the Catholic Church. It remains clear about its mission:

- Offering a faithful, monastic presence in the world;

- Providing resources and guidance to people who are seeking God through prayer and spiritual direction;

- Conducting schools that offer quality, flexible, and holistic formation for those preparing for priesthood, lay ministry, or other service in the Church and the world.

The Benedictine community currently numbers 140, including six junior monks and three novices. This makes Saint Meinrad the third largest Benedictine monastery in the United States and the sixth largest in the world.

The Archabbey's primary works are educating the Church's future leaders in its College and School of Theology and providing religious and inspirational products through Abbey Press.

The Abbey Press traces its roots to 1867 when Saint Meinrad bought a second-hand printing press and some type. Today, the Press manufactures and distributes inspirational gift items and publishes and prints a variety of books and pamphlets for the Christian family.

Saint Meinrad College and School of Theology are truly national schools, drawing their student bodies from thirty states and several foreign countries. Both Schools, with their combined enrollment of nearly 250, remain committed to their traditional work of preparing future priests for the Church while also helping to meet the Church's need for well-educated, prayerful religious and lay leaders.

With its holistic program and emphasis on personal growth, Saint Meinrad College is preparing tomorrow's Catholic leaders, lay and ordained, as few liberal arts colleges can. At Saint Meinrad School of Theology, a cooperative attitude between faculty and students, a well-designed and challenging curriculum, and a Benedictine tradition of liturgy and spirituality offer priesthood and lay students an education and formation second to none.

The quality education and formation offered at Saint Meinrad is validated each day by the leadership and service of more than 6,000 living alumni (2,000 of whom are priests) who reside in every state in the U.S. By their lives, they witness to the importance of Gospel values; by their ministry and leadership, they seek to lead others to God.

Operating the Seminary Schools is a rewarding experience for the Saint Meinrad

Benedictines. But it has been, and continues to be, financially demanding. By keeping tuition and fees affordable to dioceses, students and their families, the income generated by the Schools has not kept pace with expenses. In fact, student charges cover less than half the actual costs. The balance has been subsidized in various ways: (1) by the contributed services of the monks who work in the Schools and draw only a subsistence salary; (2) by financial contributions from other Saint Meinrad apostolates, such as the Abbey Press; and (3) by a vigorous Development Program.

Since 1967, the monks of Saint Meinrad have been inviting alumni of the Schools and other people of faith, especially those served by priest alumni, to join them as partners in the work of seminary education. They have responded prayerfully and invested generously in Saint Meinrad.

Looking to the Future

Saint Meinrad today is a vibrant institution, rooted in its 1,500 years of Benedictine tradition, yet forward-looking in its effort to serve the needs of the Church. The Benedictine community and the College and Theologate are holding steady in size. There is no long-term debt. And although the Schools have required increasing subsidies in recent years, the institution has been able to build its endowment from $5 million to $15 million during the last decade. Saint Meinrad is ready now to move forward with one of its major goals—the top priority in its recently completed 25-year institutional Master Plan—the renovation of the Archabbey Church.

The Heart of Saint Meinrad: The Archabbey Church

The Archabbey Church of Our Lady of Einsiedeln is very special to the monks of Saint Meinrad. More than an outstanding example of Romanesque architecture, more than a beloved building, more than a place where monks mark the stages of their lives from reception as novices to profession of solemn vows to passage from this life to the next, the Archabbey Church is the life-giving heart, the spiritual center, of Saint Meinrad.

This church holds special prominence for visitors, students and alumni as well. Within its sandstone walls they experience Saint Meinrad's distinguished liturgical tradition, whether through the celebration of daily Mass or the inspiring liturgies of Holy Week and the Easter Triduum. This sacred space is where they come to know the Church's round of daily prayer, where they enter into intimacy with the Mystery of God.

The Beauty of the Building

For nearly ninety years, the bells of the Archabbey Church have called monks, students and guests to an awareness of God's presence in their lives. Begun in 1899 and completed in 1907, the stately Romanesque church was designed by Br. Adrian Werwer, OFM, of St. Louis, MO. Built of hand-chiseled native sandstone, it stands as a testament to the faith, vision and perseverance of the early monks.

It is also a symbol of the partnership which has characterized Saint Meinrad through the years. Just as the monks and townspeople worked side by side to construct the 10,500-square-foot church, so, too, today they work together in furthering Saint Meinrad's apostolates.

The Archabbey Church, with its twin spires, graceful arches and rich stained glass windows, was last renovated in the late 1960s. An initial and extensive interior renovation, intended to reflect the principles of the Second Vatican Council, was begun in 1968. The parish of St. Meinrad, which had long shared the use of the Archabbey Church with the monks, had completed building its own church in 1960. So, from that point forward, the Archabbey Church no longer had to function as both a parish church and a monastic church.

A Period of Reflection

During the late '60s renovation, the monastic community decided to provide a period of reflection on the changes. The monks determined that five years would be an appropriate time to evaluate how the changes were working, how best to continue the second phase of the renovation, and how the space within the church could be further enhanced to support their prayer.

Completing the Renovation

But other commitments (the Schools, new monastery and new library) commanded the community's attention and resources. And the reflection period stretched from five years to twenty-five. Now, 140 years since the blessing of the monastery's first log cabin church, 90 years after the construction of the current church, and 25 years after completing the first phase of a planned two-phase renovation, the Benedictine community at Saint Meinrad has again turned its attention to the renovation of its most sacred space, the Archabbey Church.

The Guiding Principles of the Renovation

Although discussion about resuming the renovation of the Archabbey Church has surfaced a number of times during the past 25 years, it became formalized a year ago. At that time, Archabbot Timothy Sweeney, OSB, appointed a committee of monks to coordinate the development of theological and liturgical principles to guide the renovation.

Since then, the community has involved itself in numerous discussions, surveys and consultations with liturgical experts, engineers and an architect. These discussions resulted in several guiding principles for the renovation of Archabbey Church:

- The Archabbey Church is a sacred space and a place of prayer and worship. All aspects of the renovation shall promote and maintain an environment in which a spirit of prayer, recollection and the worthy celebration of the sacraments are encouraged.

- The Archabbey Church is, first and foremost, a monastic church. The renovation shall clearly reflect the identity and integrity of the monastic community.

- The Romanesque character of the church shall be respected.

- The construction and placement of the altar and monastic choir shall clearly represent their importance to the praying community.

♦ Because hospitality is an important value of the Benedictine tradition, the environment in the church shall encourage and facilitate guests and students joining the monks in prayer.

♦ Liturgical furnishings shall reflect the monastic values of authenticity, simplicity, stability and craftsmanship, and contribute to the beauty and elegance of the interior.

♦ The spatial arrangement shall allow for movement, flexibility, and the participation of the elderly and infirm members of the monastic community and guests.

♦ Deficiencies in heating, cooling, ventilation, lighting and sound systems shall be corrected, while the excellent acoustical properties are maintained.

These guidelines for the renovation of Archabbey Church were approved by the conventual chapter of Saint Meinrad Archabbey in January, 1994. The architectural firm of Woollen, Molzan and Partners, Indianapolis, IN, has been retained to design the renovation according to the guidelines and the currently accepted principles of ecclesial, liturgical and monastic life. The firm is experienced in church renovations as well as new church design.

The Renovation's Objectives

By undertaking this renovation, Saint Meinrad—with the help of alumni and friends—will be:

♦ Preserving a sacred space which is

  • the very heart of Saint Meinrad, the place where the very meaning of monastic life is experienced and expressed;

  • the center of Saint Meinrad, the focal point for the entire Archabbey community—monks, students, co-workers, alumni, and benefactors;

  • a defining element of Saint Meinrad, symbolizing the institution's rock-solid foundation, its tradition of partnership with neighbors and benefactors, and its aspirations, confidence and faith; and

  • a local landmark, an impressive example of Romanesque art and architecture, which represents Saint Meinrad's stability and service to the community.

♦ Enhancing the celebration of liturgy at Saint Meinrad for monks, students and guests alike.

♦ Praising God by renewing His holy temple.

Elements of the Renovation

The plan for the renovation of the Archabbey Church provides for both continuity and change. The renovated church will function well liturgically, accommodate the monastic community as well as both small and large groups of students and guests, and maintain its Romanesque character. The major elements of the renovation, as currently conceived, are as follows:

The Floor Plan

A new floor plan will respect the Archabbey Church's original architectural concept while eliminating the current system of two levels. Having the church on one level provides greater flexibility, an ease of celebration, and

better access for the elderly and physically challenged. The altar, the focal point of the church, will remain near the west entrance.

The upper level of the church will be lowered and the galleries in the transept removed. Wooden choir stalls will be placed in the transept for the monastic community. Guests will be situated west of the choir stalls in parallel rows.

The Blessed Sacrament Chapel

A new Blessed Sacrament Chapel, within the Archabbey Church, will form an integral part of the overall design of the church. This chapel will be larger than the present temporary chapel and clearly communicate a sense of reverence.

Plans include the use of at least part of the old gold altar, which had been in the apse of the Archabbey Church prior to the 1960s renovation. This ornate altar, made in Bavaria of gold, enamel and semi-precious stones, is currently housed in the crypt of the church.

The Windows

Natural and artificial light are important to the overall scheme of the renovated Archabbey Church. The lower windows of the church, which depict the Beatitudes and various saints, will be preserved, repaired and cleaned. The beauty of these painted glass windows made in 1908 in the Munich, Germany, studio of Francis X. Zettler, will be enhanced.

The Shrine of Our Lady of Einsiedeln

A shrine honoring Our Lady of Einsiedeln, the patroness of the Archabbey Church, will be erected in a place of prominence within the church. Here will stand the revered statue of Our Lady of Einsiedeln, given to Saint Meinrad Archabbey by its mother abbey, Maria Einsiedeln, on the 100th anniversary of the Archabbey.

The Organ

The massive pipe organ, rebuilt in the early 1960s from the original Estey organ, will remain the primary musical instrument in the church. The pipeworks located in the north gallery will be relocated to the apse to provide greater clarity of tone and ease of accompaniment.

The Floor

The floor of a Romanesque church is typically one of the more striking features of the building. The present concrete and carpeted floor will be replaced with beautiful and durable marble or stone.

The perspective of this rendering, from the west side of the Archabbey Church, shows the interior as one level. In the far back, in the apse, is the striking Christus, painted by the Belgian monk, Fr. Gregory deWit, OSB. The altar will be situated on the west side of the church, near the main doors. Although many details still remain to be decided, this rendering captures the openness, simple beauty, and Romanesque lines of the renovated Archabbey Church.

Furnishings

Furnishings selected for the Archabbey Church will harmonize with its interior design. All will strive to reflect the monastic values and practices of authenticity, simplicity, stability and craftsmanship.

The Mechanical Systems

The present mechanical systems in the Archabbey Church are clearly inadequate. Very little upgrading of them has taken place since the church was built nearly 90 years ago. A new electrical system is needed, as are lighting, sound, heating and air-conditioning systems. The present acoustics of the church are considered excellent and will be maintained, if not enhanced.

The Structure of the Building

As with any aging building, improvements and repairs are needed to keep the structure in excellent condition. In the Archabbey Church renovation, a drainage problem along the foundation of the nave wall will be corrected. The exterior stone will be tuck-pointed and the roof insulated.

Additionally, the gold crosses and fleurs-de-lis will be regilded. In the distinctive Archabbey Church towers, the clocks will be repaired and Bell Number Six, which cracked in 1973, will be recast or replaced.

The Outdoor Plaza and Landscaping

The physical space around the exterior of the Archabbey Church is an extension of the environment inside. To make it more welcoming and to provide for a better transition to the sacred space inside, a plaza will be built immediately outside the west, or main, entrance to the church. Once the renovation is complete, guests will be encouraged to enter the church through the west doors.

This plan for the Archabbey Church lays out a direction in which the renovation work will develop. As with any project of this size and scope, details of the plan remain to be worked out. Decisions about such things as color, proportion, type and extent of ornamentation and furnishings will be carefully made by the monastic community in consultation with the architect. Since these decisions still need to be made, some elements of this renovation plan may be readdressed to assure continuity of style and purpose.

While incorporating the many perspectives that have emerged during the community's year-long discussions about the renovation, the plan also provides for both continuity and change. It reflects Saint Meinrad's valued tradition of preserving its heritage while looking to the future with faith, hope and confidence.

This drawing reflects the placement of the organ in the apse, the monastic choir in the transept and guest seating to the west of the choir. All furniture used in the renovation will reflect the monastic tradition of authenticity, simplicity, and craftsmanship. With the opening of the transept, natural light, too, will become a stronger element of the church's interior environment.

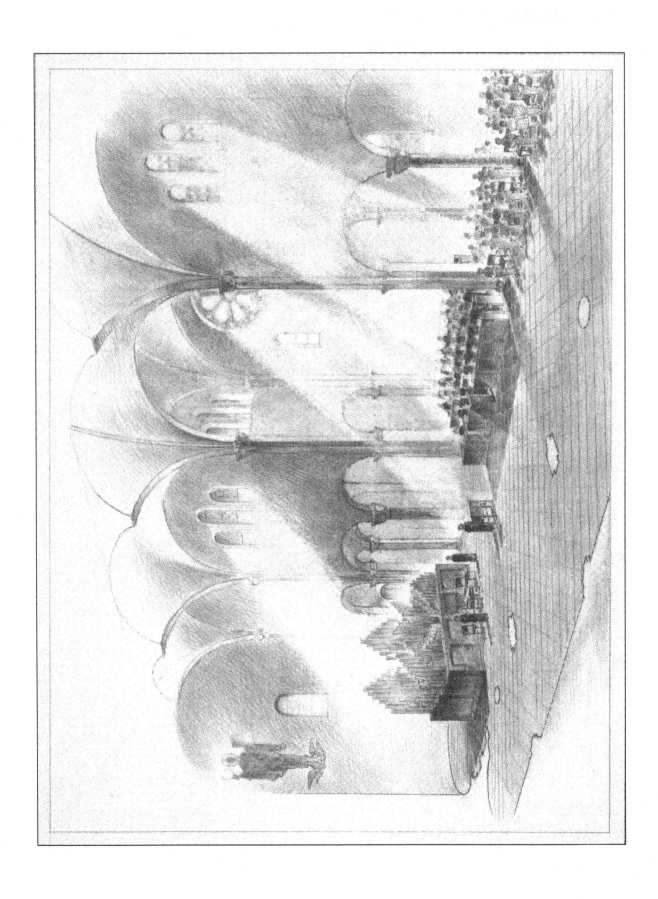

Funding the Renovation

The projected cost of renovating the Archabbey Church is $4.5 million. Included in this figure are all the costs associated with repairing, renovating, and furnishing the church.

Although the projected cost of this renovation is substantial, very little has been spent on the Archabbey Church since it was constructed in 1907. Even the 1968 renovation was accomplished at minimal expense. For all practical purposes, the heating, electrical, and lighting systems have not been updated in 90 years. The replacement value of the church, based on the size, style and quality of the Archabbey Church today, is estimated to be $8.5 million.

Presently on hand for the renovation of the church is $1 million. Most of this fund has come from bequests, many from relatives of monks. With this beginning, an additional $3.5 million is needed to realize the goals set forth in the renovation plan.

An Invitation to Make a Difference

In the past, the monks of Saint Meinrad have invited others to assist with the funding of capital projects. Alumni and friends have responded generously. For this reason, the monks of Saint Meinrad are confident that others will want to join them in renovating the Archabbey Church. They plan to extend that opportunity to alumni and friends during the next year.

Of course, Saint Meinrad recognizes that the success of this venture depends on the very generous investment of a few: a small group of leaders who have manifested a special interest in the Archabbey Church. It is this group of devoted friends who will be given the opportunity to lead the renewal and renovation of Saint Meinrad's cherished House of the Lord. These special benefactors know and appreciate the significance of this church in the lives of the Benedictine monks, students, alumni, and benefactors of Saint Meinrad, and in their own lives.

For nearly ninety years, monks and guests have celebrated the Liturgy of the Hours in the Archabbey Church. With the help of generous friends, monks and others will continue to gather in Archabbey Church four times a day, 365 days a year, to praise God in prayer, song and sacrament.

Commemorative Opportunities

In accomplishing the renovation of Archabbey Church, there will be several opportunities to memorialize loved ones. Commemorative opportunities in Saint Meinrad's House of the Lord are a fitting way to honor beloved family members, friends, or monks, and to express gratitude to God for abundant blessings.

The Commemorative Opportunities listed below are available on a first pledge basis. Donors and/or those to be honored or memorialized will be appropriately recognized in the renovated church or the plaza outside the main entrance to the church.

(The suggested minimum gift for a commemoration does not necessarily reflect the actual cost of that item but it does suggest its significance in accomplishing the goals of the renovation of the Archabbey Church.)

Commemorative Item	Suggested Minimum Gift
Blessed Sacrament Chapel	$500,000
New Marble or Stone Floor	500,000
Heating, Venting and Air-Conditioning System	500,000
Relocation of the Organ and Pipeworks	400,000
Wooden Choir Stalls	300,000
Outdoor Plaza (west of the church)	250,000
New Lighting System	200,000
New Sound System (with an audio loop for the hearing impaired)	200,000
Shrine of Our Lady of Einsiedeln	100,000
Restoration of the Stained Glass Windows	100,000
Renovation of the Crypt (as a chapel for Byzantine and other liturgies)	100,000
Guest Seating	100,000
Altar, Ambo (lectern) and Presider's Chair	100,000
Altar in the Blessed Sacrament Chapel	75,000
Replacement of Bell Number Six	75,000
Regilding of the Gold Crosses and Fleurs-de-Lis	50,000
Repair of the Tower Clocks	50,000
Landscaping	25,000
St. Meinrad Shrine	25,000
Courtyard Outside the Blessed Sacrament Chapel	25,000
New West Entrance Doors	25,000

A Most Worthwhile Endeavor

The renovation of the Archabbey Church is more than just the renewal of a church building. It also involves the renewal of individuals, a community, and an institution.

Saint Meinrad's Archabbey Church symbolizes, in a physical and enduring way, faith in God's abiding presence in individual lives; a community's devotion to its prayer and worship; and an institution's confidence in and commitment to the future. This splendid sandstone church truly is the heart of Saint Meinrad. From it flows the meaning of and motivation for everything that Saint Meinrad is and does.

Because the Archabbey Church plays such a central role in the life of Saint Meinrad, the decision to move forward with its renovation has been made only after much prayer, reflection and consultation. During the past year, the monastic community carefully reviewed a host of considerations—theological, liturgical, aesthetic, practical—related to the renovation of this monastic church. With the conviction that God will bless their efforts, the Benedictine community has made the decision to resume and complete, here and now, the renovation begun a quarter of a century ago.

Indeed, $4.5 million is a substantial investment. Yet that investment must be weighed in light of the impact it will have on the monks, students, alumni, and guests who will be drawn closer to God by their prayer in the Archabbey Church. It must also consider what the church symbolizes about Saint Meinrad and witnesses to the world: God's constant presence in our lives, the centrality of prayer, and the treasured tradition of monks and townspeople/benefactors joined together in prayer and work. And it must recognize the Archabbey Church's role as a prominent landmark in southern Indiana—a source of pride to local citizens, a symbol of strength and stability, a beacon of hope.

Asking God's blessing on the work of renovating the Archabbey Church, the monks of Saint Meinrad invite you to participate generously in this most worthwhile endeavor. And they pray that in this renewal of Saint Meinrad's nearly century-old House of the Lord, as in all things, *God may be glorified*.

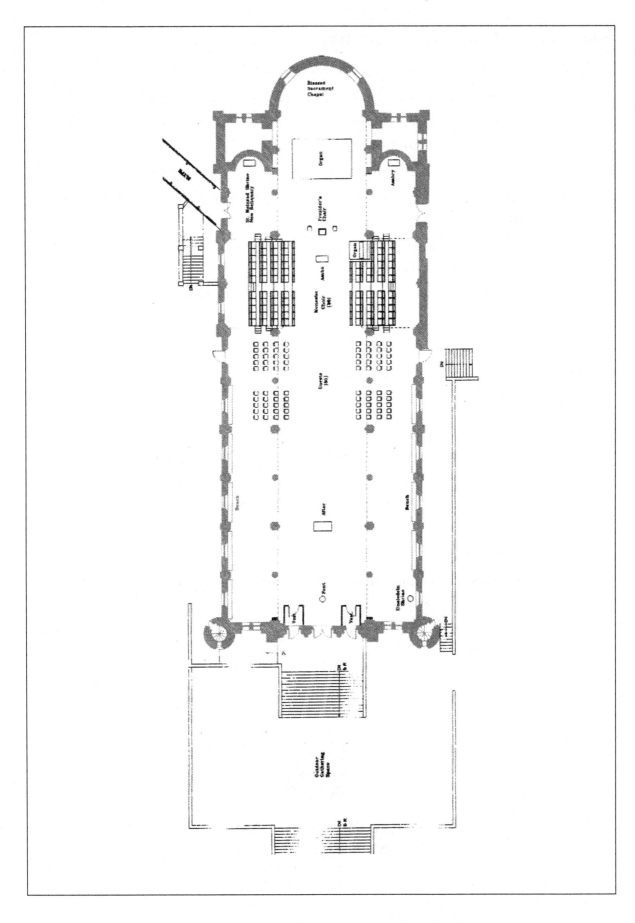

Milestones in Saint Meinrad's History

1854   Saint Meinrad founded by the Swiss Abbey of Maria Einsiedeln.

1857   Monks establish and staff a school offering secondary education.

1861   Seminary school curriculum expanded to include courses in the classics, commerce, philosophy and theology.

1867   Used printing press purchased—the forerunner of Abbey Press.

1870   Saint Meinrad raised to an independent abbey. Martin Marty, OSB, elected first abbot.

1878   Subiaco Abbey, the first of five monasteries to be founded by Saint Meinrad, established in Arkansas.

1887   A great fire destroys the monastery, seminary and church building.

1890   St. Joseph Abbey in Louisiana established by Saint Meinrad.

1899   Construction of the Archabbey Church begun.

1907   Archabbey Church completed and dedicated to Our Lady of Einsiedeln.

1933   Marmion Abbey in Illinois founded by Saint Meinrad.

1950   Blue Cloud Abbey established by Saint Meinrad in South Dakota.

1954   Saint Meinrad named an Archabbey—one of only seven in the world.

1958   Prince of Peace Abbey founded by Saint Meinrad in southern California.

1968   Initial renovation of the Archabbey Church begun.

1979 $7.5 million campaign for construction of monastery and library buildings launched.

1994   Monastic community announces plan to complete the renovation of the Archabbey Church.

Saint Meinrad Archabbey
St. Meinrad, IN 47577-1025
1-800-682-0988

Letter Sent to "Insiders" During Renovation

August 2, 1996

Dear _____,

Each July 16 is a very special day at Saint Meinrad: the Feast of Our Lady of Einsiedeln, patroness of our Archabbey Church. It is a day that honors our kind and loving Mother and brings together in prayer the Saint Meinrad community—monks, summer session students and alumni, co-workers and, this year, many Benedictines from around the country who were here for a Study Week. This year, the Feast of Our Lady of Einsiedeln was no different from years before, except for one thing. We gathered for worship in the School of Theology Chapel rather than the Archabbey Church.

As you probably know, the Archabbey Church is undergoing renovation and renewal. The construction crews began in earnest in June and, at periods during the day, the ruckus of jackhammer and falling concrete echo throughout the Archabbey. Sometimes the volume of dust flying out the front doors looks a bit like a snowstorm. It's all part of the process.

This point in the renewal of the Archabbey Church has been a long time in coming. As a community we've waited, and we've dickered, and we've come to consensus on many difficult decisions. Now people watch the slow progress, day-by-day. They're anxious for the calendar days to pass and will be glad to see the finished product.

Our friends, students and alumni support the renovation effort and many have helped us pay for the work. We are very grateful for such generosity and involvement. In talking with these people, I've found that the significance of the Archabbey Church in their lives is every bit as valued and strong as it is in the lives of the monks. We monks have gathered for prayer within that magnificent building four times a day, season in and season out, for nearly a hundred years. Over the years, these special friends have joined us every chance they've had. As we monks lift up our prayer, these people are especially remembered—whether they're physically with us or not. These generous souls are living testimony of the works of Saint Meinrad and our ministry to the Catholic Church.

For us Benedictines, who have pledged to make this geographic spot our home for life, the Archabbey Church is the heart of our community. Prayer, both communal and solitary, is our chief undertaking. Being able to lift up our voices within a structure built by the sweat and labor of a generation of our monk-predecessors and townspeople, a building that by its simple beauty glorifies the gifts of the Almighty, that means so much to us. The place is important to the prayer—and by enhancing the place, we enhance our prayer.

Archabbot Lambert Reilly, OSB   *Saint Meinrad*   St. Meinrad, Indiana 47577
Archabbey

While the renovation is underway, we monks gather in a small tent-like structure that was erected in our monastery courtyard. We were blessed in securing this structure because we got a good price on the materials. It was masterfully put up by the talents of our crews from the physical plant, and once we're back inside our re-dedicated Archabbey Church, the structure's materials can be sold.

It's a quaint little building, and it's working out even better than we had anticipated. The intimate size brings us closer together physically. It will teach us to be patient with each other; it will build up the anticipation of what is to come. The contrast of what we had and what we now have may open our hearts to the glory of what is to come. We have to be a little less dramatic in our celebrations right now, we limit our movement, and sometimes we have to use other spaces for our prayer—such as the Schools' chapels for larger events—but these temporary conditions remind us that our lives are really just lived out from day to day, until the real worship in eternal liturgy comes.

The size of the renovation chapel limits how many guests can join us in prayer, and that is a concern for us. But the fully renovated Archabbey Church will rectify the situation, as it will bring our guests closer to all that we do in prayer. We consider you, our guests, members of our extended family. Although we don't take you into the cloistered area, we do take you into our hearts and the heart of what we do here—praying as the voice of the Church. Your presence is a vital element in our work as monks. We very much look forward to having you physically with us again.

In addition to the physical aspects of the renovation, a communal renewal is subtly taking place. If you look into the liturgy that surrounds the commemoration of a church, you'll see that almost all of the prayers and the Scriptures talk about our being built from living stones. In other words, if a "church raising" doesn't build community, then the church is just a museum. So, as the struggle is undertaken to build and fortify the Archabbey Church, there is sort of a cementing of us, the builders, occurring. While we might not be physically involved in the work, we and the people who have been so generous in making possible the physical renovation are the living stones that will build the church. We're building up the body of Christ.

And so, even as we gather for special feast days, and monastic commemorations, and professions and funerals in spaces other than our beloved Archabbey Church, we all participate in a magnificent renewal. Both physically and spiritually, the work of renovation affects us all. We are joined in the anticipation of the glory—both physical and spiritual—that is yet to come.

I ask you to keep us in your prayers . . . and I promise that we will do the same for you.

Yours in the Lord,

Major Leaders Dinner: Palm Beach, Florida, February 26, 1994

One of the distinguishing characteristics of Benedictines is their vow of stability. In a 10th-century vita, or life, of St. Meinrad, which is read every year at the Abbey on January 21, we read that St. Meinrad on seeing a certain spot in the now Swiss forest immediately knew that this was the spot for him. St. Meinrad, the author says, immediately fell in love with the place. According to the 10th-century monastic author, this "falling in love" with the place was a very common occurrence. It was, and is, a sign of Benedictine vocation, of a call from God, for this individual.

Ten centuries later the Benedictine of St. Meinrad continues to "fall in love" with the people, the regular Divine Praise, the seminary work, the Conventual Mass, the view out the Belvedere of the monastery, the Abbey Church, the morning sun breaking through the pines as we leave choir after Morning Office. It's all of these people, buildings, work, views and sights together, not always seen and expressed clearly, but certainly felt deeply by all at St. Meinrad. When a man commits himself for life as a Benedictine with this stability of place, you can be sure there's a love affair going on.

Of all the buildings, work, people, and views at St. Meinrad, the one outstanding "signature," the "John Hancock" of St. Meinrad, is the Archabbey Church. For the Benedictine monks of St. Meinrad this edifice is more than just one of many "loved" buildings at the abbey. The Abbey Church is the structure where the monks mark the stages of their lives: reception as a novice, vows, ordination, and burial liturgy. This church marks the heart of St. Meinrad, pumping out life-giving nourishment to all that happens at St. Meinrad. Even for our students and alumni the church marks the place where they were ordained as deacons or priests. It's the place where almost by osmosis they imbibe the Benedictine round of daily prayer. Whether or not you've come to the Abbey Church for office or the Eucharist or whether or not you've come to know any of the monks, there is one thing at St. Meinrad you can't avoid—the bells! Whether you like them or not, you can't totally avoid them. On first arriving at St. Meinrad the student or guest is awakened from sleep by the bells, or at another time they might cause the student or guest to mumble: "*Now* what are they ringing the bells for!!" After a few days you get used to them, and you find that the bells have faded from your awareness. But even then, periodically, they interrupt you. The bells *alone* remind student or guest of one thing that is now and always will be necessary for our lives: prayer—fixed, daily prayer. Each of us needs that daily intimacy with the Mystery of God in which we live. The Archabbey Church at St. Meinrad is somewhat like a large family room at Christmas or Thanksgiving. It's within those church walls that the real meaning and heart of St. Meinrad pumps.

That's why we've begun planning for the renovation of the Abbey Church. What was begun at St. Meinrad as a 9×12 log cabin church, with Father Jerome Backman writing to the

Abbot of Einsiedeln in 1854, ". . . on March 14th I offered the first Mass to God and Mary, and our patron, St. Meinrad," this log cabin church progressed to a 75×45 frame church 3 years later in 1857. It wasn't until 1899 that work on the present structure was begun, and according to the construction timetable of the time, the present church was solemnly blessed 8 years later in 1907. Some of you are aware that following Vatican Council II, in 1968, we began what was to be an *initial* phase of the renovation of the Abbey Church, to be taken up again in 1972, but a little over 25 years later we're only now turning our attention back to the most important part of St. Meinrad. As in any family or living institution, plans get changed. For us there was the renovation of Benet Hall in 1968 that focused our attention; then the new monastery and library in 1982, and, just recently, St. Anselm Hall in 1990. It's now abundantly clear that the electrical system, heating, some foundation work, and other physical plant items need attention, not to mention the whole aesthetic look of the interior of our church.

But I also think there was a more subtle, less coherent reason, for our delay. When any of us is dealing with something we consider terribly important, we hesitate, almost by habit, before making our decisions. Since the Abbey Church at St. Meinrad is the heart, the pump, of all of St. Meinrad, then this hesitation, this period of reflection, was almost a given, what with all the required changes and their swiftness following Vatican Council II. Yet our original period of reflection, from the initial work done in 1968 in which we tried to implement some of the changes required by Vatican Council II, coupled, as we thought then, with a 5-year reflection period, has now stretched into a 20-year "reflection" period. For some this might seem a long period of time, 20 years, and even for some of the monks there were, how should I say, "manifestations of impatience," but I must remind you, as I have reminded the monks, that for a Benedictine, for weal or woe, 20 years is really not a long period of time; that's only one generation, and when you're taught to develop a view of events and decisions not in terms of years but decades and centuries, one generation of thought might just be the right amount. It's not a very American way of doing things, but there you have it . . . a certain conflict between American and Benedictine ways of doing things.

However one views the past, the die has now been cast. We at St. Meinrad are ready and willing to renovate our Abbey Church. Early last August we began our discussions and these have been followed by subsequent discussions and some decisions. As always these types of decisions move from the more general to the more specific. We've established a Program Document—the "more general"—and just a week ago, on February 19, began moving to the "more specific." Let me move somewhat in the same manner, from the more general to the more specific.

Of course, deficiencies in lighting, sound, heating and venting systems are to be corrected, with the installation of some form of air-conditioning especially for the hot, humid southern Indiana summers. Much more important is our desire to preserve the basic Romanesque structure of our Abbey Church. The Romanesque style of architecture is often called the monastic style, very much influenced in the 10th and 11th centuries by monasticism. Often enough, and fairly enough, people view St. Meinrad as a specialized educational institution in our Church. We've been preparing men for the priesthood for over 140 years, and for at least the last 25 years, lay ministers. Indeed, when St. Meinrad was established in 1854 one of its prime purposes was this education of the clergy. Yet what we have not spoken of so frequently, verbally or in print, is that another of the basic reasons in 1854 for the establishment of St. Meinrad was as a possible refuge for the monks of Einsiedeln should the secularizing tendencies of the 19th century spread into Switzerland and the government close Einsiedeln. It was important for the monks of Einsiedeln to have a possible refuge so that monastic life could continue. In and of itself monastic life is a value for our Church, a vocation in our Church that has an independence from whatever work the monks undertake. The monks want you to know that the Abbey Church is first and foremost a monastic church, following our historic lineage. Today, one area in a Catholic Church that is highlighted is the baptistry. You don't now, and really won't in the future, find a baptistry in the Archabbey Church. You'll certainly find holy water in the future renovated church, but baptism is reserved, if you will, for the parish church. As in the present church at St. Meinrad, so in the future renovation, you'll find a choir, the area where the monks gather four times a day to pray the Divine Office and celebrate the Eucharist. In general, you do not find a section in a parish church with choir stalls.

As you might well expect, we see the renovated church to be a sacred space, a space for prayer and worship, with the Eucharist, and hence the altar, to have the prominent place. One's eyes on entering the renovated Abbey Church—not from the present side entrances, but from the main doors of the Abbey Church—should move almost immediately to the altar. The atmosphere of our renovated Abbey Church should encourage quiet and prayer, with furnishings that reflect our monastic values of authenticity, simplicity, stability and craftsmanship, and a Blessed Sacrament chapel that manifests the respect and dignity of the presence of our God among us. Since we sing so much of the Divine Office and the Eucharist at St. Meinrad, and music plays an important part of our lives, we consider that the question of acoustics is a most important consideration. We're blessed at present by having basically good acoustics, and we don't want the renovation to ruin or impede the solid quality of the acoustics in the church. Finally, our guests. As a general principle we at St. Meinrad want our renovated church to reflect our traditional hospitality to our guests. We want to enable those who visit St. Meinrad to participate in the Divine Office and especially the Eucharist and those who simply come to observe what we do (we do have any number of non-Catholic visitors) to be able to do this while respecting the needs and the nature of a Roman Catholic liturgy celebrated in a monastic setting.

The Program Document, the general principles, has been established; the architect chosen, Evans Woollen of Indianapolis, who has worked with us in the construction of the new monastery and library and the renovation of the old monastery into St. Anselm Hall; and, as of February 19, last Saturday, we've begun the slow process of moving from the general to the specific. We spent all last Saturday working on this and have arrived at certain clearer proposals. It is being suggested that (1) there will be only one basic level to the church, not as at present where, as some of you know, the church is divided into two distinct levels, one raised about 7 feet above the other. This one level is certainly more in line with a traditional Romanesque church and in addition provides much better for those who have difficulty in climbing all those steps. (2) The monks' choir will be tiered, that is, the rows will be slightly raised, one just a little higher than the other. Each side of the choir will be so arranged. (3) We are also considering opening the transepts, the two balconies which face each other, one on the north side and the other on the south side. Taking out these transepts will more clearly restore the church to its Romanesque cruciform, or crucifix, shape, while at the same time permitting more natural light to enter the church through the large window now blocked by organ pipes. And, as of last Saturday, that's as far as we've gotten . . . officially! I do see us returning to some form of choir stall; of providing a more fitting Blessed Sacrament chapel; and having a more permanent, stable altar. Not much so far, but I think that by late spring/early summer of this year we will have a schematic design, a picture of what the renovated Abbey Church will look like. In the meantime the architect will be bringing down to us several rough sketches of what we proposed to him last Saturday, and we'll be meeting throughout this spring to hammer out the specifics.

We at St. Meinrad have set aside some funds for this renovation. Since it is first and foremost the monks' church, I have been setting aside some of the inheritances received by the monks from their families. We don't have enough of ourselves and we don't intend to launch into some kind of public campaign. We plan to invite a limited number of our benefactors to help us realize this dream of completing the renovation of our Abbey Church. I think that our original timetable is still in place to begin the actual renovation in late 1995 or early 1996.

When I announced last year my impending resignation in June 1995, I did indicate that one of my goals before resigning was to get this renovation of the Abbey Church underway. Just as Abbot Gabriel, my predecessor, bequeathed to me the planning for the new monastery, library, and renovation back in 1978, I hope to bequeath to my successor the funds and the plans for the actual renovation of the Abbey Church. This church and what goes on in it touches the heart and center of what St. Meinrad is all about. Who we are and what we do for our Church is focused and centered in this sacred space. By our renovation of this sacred space we, I think, demonstrate again that although drawing heavily from our past, and living fully in the present, we are always looking to the future with confidence in our God-given abilities and in the ever present Spirit who guides our Church, St. Meinrad, and each of us. It is certainly my hope that many of you will help us renew this House of God. Among all the buildings and works carried on at St. Meinrad, this edifice and the praise of God that goes on in it speaks to the heart and center of St. Meinrad.

Thanks for coming this evening, and I'll keep you posted as our plans progress.

+Timothy, OSB

Prayerfully Renovating a Sacred Space

*"If the Lord does not build the house,
in vain do its builders labor. . . ."*

Psalm 126

"We monks are here because of those before us. We must preserve the riches we've been given, add to them, and make them available to future generations." Fr. Kurt Stasiak, OSB, with enthusiasm and conviction, discusses the upcoming renovation of the Archabbey Church. "This is *our* Church," he says, "our 'sacred space,' not just any church."

Fr. Kurt chairs the committee charged with planning the renovation, which approached the process with great care. "Our main goal was to reflect the views of 140 monks, in age from 23 to 95, who worship five times a day in this Church."

Joining Fr. Kurt on the Archabbey Church Renovation Committee are Fr. Aurelius Boberek, Fr. Colman Grabert, Fr. Warren Heitz, Fr. Harry Hagan, and Br. Adrian Burke, secretary. The renovation planning began in September 1993.

Throughout the planning process, two overriding emotions surfaced within the committee members: honor and humility. "It has been a privilege for us to be a part of this significant work," admits Fr. Kurt. "This is not just another task for us; it is a sacred trust." He believes their decisions had to address how each of the monks treasures his "sacred space."

The renovation's significance, he adds, is that it speaks of tradition, preserves history, enhances a local landmark, and means a great deal to the monks and to the regional community of faithful.

Guiding Principles

Three years ago, former Archabbot Timothy Sweeney, OSB, appointed this committee to complete a renovation begun in the 1960s. He charged them with developing theological and liturgical principles to guide this major undertaking. First and foremost among the guiding principles approved by the monastic chapter in January 1994 is that the Archabbey Church is a *monastic* church. The renovation shall clearly reflect the identity and integrity of the monastic community.

The other principles are:

♦ All aspects of the renovation shall promote and maintain an environment in which a spirit of prayer, recollection and the worthy celebration of the sacraments are encouraged.

♦ The construction and placement of the altar and monastic choir stalls shall represent the importance of the community's prayer life.

"Monastic choir stalls visually speak of stability and permanence. They are a distinguishing characteristic of a monastic community," says Fr. Kurt. "The altar is the primary symbol of all worship. Movement around the altar will gather together those present in prayer."

♦ Hospitality is a valued Benedictine tradition. The environment shall encourage guests and students in joining the monks in prayer.

Throughout Saint Meinrad's history the monks have invited others to pray with them, alongside them, not to simply observe them.

Saint Meinrad

6

- The spatial arrangement shall allow for movement and flexibility and the participation of the elderly and infirm members of the community and guests.

  "One of the strengths of our community is how our elderly and infirm members want to stay involved. We care for their medical and physical needs, as well as facilitating their participation in the community's prayer life." The availability of battery-operated headsets for the hearing impaired is one example of how this principle can be enacted.

- Liturgical furnishings in the church shall reflect the monastic values of authenticity, simplicity, stability and craftsmanship and contribute to the beauty and elegance of the interior.

- Deficiencies in the heating, cooling, lighting and sound systems shall be corrected.

  In the past ninety years, these deficiencies have been given limited attention. By addressing these inadequacies, the renovation will enhance liturgies.

Community Commitment
"This planning process has mirrored the benefits and difficulties of community living. There have been disappointments, joys, doubts, and give and take," reflects Fr. Kurt. "The process has been a learning experience for everyone."

The monastic chapter, which met 20 times for renovation discussions, has approved all major facets of the renewal.

The Heart of Saint Meinrad

The Archabbey Church of Our Lady of Einsiedeln is very special to the monks of Saint Meinrad. More than an outstanding example of Romanesque architecture, or a beloved building, or a place where the monks mark the stages of their lives—from reception as a novice to solemn profession of vows to the funeral liturgy—the Archabbey Church is the life-giving heart, the spiritual center, of Saint Meinrad.

This church holds special prominence for visitors, friends, students and alumni as well. Within its sandstone walls they experience Saint Meinrad's distinguished liturgical tradition and come to know the Catholic Church's round of daily prayer and the celebration of the liturgical year at daily Mass.

For nearly ninety years, Archabbey Church bells have called monks, students and guests to an awareness of God's presence in their lives. Completed in 1907, the stately Archabbey Church was built of hand-chiseled native sandstone. It stands as a testament to the faith, perseverance and vision of Saint Meinrad's early monks.

It is also a symbol of the partnership with the faithful that has characterized Saint Meinrad through the years. Just as the monks and townspeople worked side by side to construct the Church, so today they work together to further Saint Meinrad's apostolates.

With prayerful discernment and much care, the monastic community has planned a rejuvenation of the Archabbey Church that will enhance all that transpires within its nearly century-old walls. The process has been a journey of faith and commitment. It reflects well Saint Meinrad's long history of *ora et labora*.

Saint Meinrad

Two things were most evident during the chapter meetings, says Fr. Kurt: the monks felt comfortable in offering their opinions and they have come to realize the complexity of the renovation.

The monastic chapter cast 10 votes for significant renovation elements, the final vote on October 1995. The committee is now finalizing the renovation details with Archabbot Lambert Reilly, OSB, and the architectural firm of Woollen, Molzan and Partners of Indianapolis, IN.

The church renovation is expected to begin in mid-April, with the dismantling of the organ. During the renovation, the community will worship in a temporary structure that has been erected in the monastery courtyard. Fr. Kurt says this was the least disruptive option for the community, and it will accommodate a small number of guests for liturgies.

Gratitude and Generosity

The renovation underscores the importance of the Archabbey Church in the lives of the monks. Yet they know this project can not happen without the generosity and conviction of the many faithful away from "the Hill." As a result, from the start, the monks approached the project with gratitude.

Fr. Kurt acknowledges that some might think initiating such a large-scale renovation is presumptuous. But for 140 years, the monks have witnessed the many blessings given them by people from all walks of life. "They share our lives, our commitment,"

Using technology to visualize the future

One of the most challenging aspects of a project the magnitude of the Archabbey Church renovation is visualizing the proposed changes in order to respond informedly. Monastic renovation committee member Fr. Harry Hagan, OSB, used modern technology to help the community understand better some of the design proposals.

"People had difficulty with visualizing the changes, understanding what the church would look like," says Fr. Harry, "particularly when the upper level is removed. This technology let them see how that space would be."

Using a computer, 3-D modeling software and videotape equipment, Fr. Harry invested more than 100 hours during the discussion phase of planning to create images in three dimensions showing the community what to expect from certain design scenarios.

Generating the images involved complicated, numerically based data entry. "The middle of the west doors at the bottom is a point known as 0–0–0. Everything in the church—the walls, floor, furnishings—has a coordinate, X-Y-Z, with X being left to right, Y being how high something begins and ends and Z being how far from the door the object is." Putting all of this data into the computer took immense detailed attention, but Fr. Harry says it proved very useful.

In one instance, the community had reservations about the proposed plan to move the organ into the apse of the church. With the 3-D creation, the community discovered the initial proposal would have obscured the Christus, a very unpopular outcome.

So the architect came back with another idea that has been more workable. "The 3-D work was time well-spent because it provided the process for a new solution to the problem."

Saint Meinrad

Fr. Kurt says. "If there is a presumption, it's that we believe those who invest in our work and prayer do so because Saint Meinrad means so much to them. Our prayers and work are our gifts back to them."

The renovation is expected to cost $4.5 to $4.8 million, yet the project has already been funded through gifts and pledges from friends, alumni, corporations and foundations. Of the total raised, $1 million came from bequests to monks from family and friends.

Some friends showed their interest by underwriting specific renovation elements, such as the Shrine of St. Meinrad and the stained glass windows. Saint Meinrad's alumni contributed to a special appeal to renovate the church towers. Their support will repair the clocks and replace a cracked bell.

Fr. Kurt feels supporters of the renovation have communicated something very special to the Benedictine community. "We feel humbled, energized and renewed by the trust people have demonstrated by their investment in this project. We're so grateful for their support of us and in the works we undertake for the Catholic Church."

Bids are currently being taken for the renovation work. If everything remains on schedule, the community hopes to be wor-

---

The Archabbey Church at a glance

- 64 feet wide and 184 feet long; from floor to the cross-vaults: 58 feet high; the towers stand at 164 feet, and the interior is 10,500 square feet.

- The spires are covered with copper, the rest of the roof with slate.

- The two-and-a-half- to three-foot thick walls are made of hand-cut Saint Meinrad sandstone. The sandstone was transported by mule from the quarry at Monte Cassino.

- The stained glass windows in the crypt and along the roof of the church were made in St. Louis. The lower windows of the church, depicting the Beatitudes and Benedictine saints, and the two in the apse came from Munich.

- The original organ contained 3 manuals, 55 ranks and 3,015 pipes. It was inaugurated on the first anniversary of the dedication of the Archabbey Church (March 21, 1908). It was replaced in the 1960s with an organ that has 3 manuals plus pedals. This will be redesigned in the renovation to have 60 ranks and more than 3,000 pipes.

- The newly built church's main (gold) altar was made in Bavaria. Patterned after a shrine in the Cologne Cathedral, the gold and enamel altar is inlaid with semi-precious stones. This altar, in part, will be located in the renovated Blessed Sacrament Chapel.

- Originally, a gallery stretched 14 feet from the west wall, above the main entrance. To avoid sacrificing interior space, Abbot Athanasius had the architect design two round towers, flanking the façade, to house stairs to the gallery. As enrollment increased, a second gallery was installed. Both were removed in the renovation of the 1960s.

- The initial cost of the construction at the turn of the century was $50,000, not including the material and labor supplied by the Abbey.

Saint Meinrad

shipping in their renovated church within 12 to 15 months.

"Success in the renovation of our 'sacred space' will come," nods Fr. Kurt, "from the generosity of others, our own hard work and, above all, the grace of God."

The History of the Archabbey Church

Planning and excavation began in the 1890s, under Abbot Fintan Mundwiler, OSB. The actual construction was completed in nearly eight years under Abbot Athanasius Schmitt, OSB.

Excavation of the site began in 1895; the first stone was laid June 16, 1899. Bishop Denis O'Donaghue, Auxiliary Bishop of Indianapolis, blessed and laid the cornerstone on August 15, 1900. The church was under roof by 1904.

Designed by Br. Adrian Werwer, OFM, of St. Louis, the church construction was directed and supervised by Fr. Benno Gerber, OSB. Br. Joseph Schaeuble, OSB, created the patterns for the stonework and devised the timberwork for the roofs and steeples.

On March 21, 1907, the feast of St. Benedict, the community entered the church in procession for the first time. Abbot Athanasius blessed the church.

The Abbey Church was the site for liturgies for the monks, local parishioners and the students of the major and minor seminary for fifty years. In the late 1950s, the parishioners built their own church building, students began holding their liturgies in chapels within the Schools, and the Abbey Church returned to being a monastic liturgical space.

In 1968, the Benedictine community at Saint Meinrad began renovating the Archabbey Church to reflect the principles of the Second Vatican Council. After a period of experimentation with proposed changes, the community decided to "live with" the most preferred option for five years before finalizing their plans. The time frame was elongated as other institutional building projects became higher priorities. In 1993, Archabbot Timothy Sweeney, OSB, appointed a committee to oversee the completion of the renovation.

Appeal Letter Sent to Summer Session Alumni

Saint Meinrad Alumni Association

ST. MEINRAD, INDIANA 47577-1025 / 812: 357-6501
800: 682-0988
FAX: 812: 357-6759

September 12, 1995

Dear _____ ,

The Summer Session program at Saint Meinrad has been a special blessing for people like you and me. Through this set of courses, we have been able to enrich our lives and, in some cases, pursue degrees that might otherwise have been beyond our reach.

Each summer the Archabbey Church has stood on the Hill, welcoming us to our studies. The church towers stood out above the countryside, the bells calling us in to study and to prayer.

Saint Meinrad has embarked on a worthwhile project to renovate the Archabbey Church. One special component of this project is the refurbishment of the towers, including the clocks and bells. As you may know, Bell Number Six cracked in 1978; it will be replaced. The gold crosses and fleurs-de-lis will be regilded, the clocks re-worked, and the stonework tuck-pointed. In all, this will be a major effort.

The Alumni Associations have taken up the challenge of raising the $100,000 needed to fund this part of the renovation project. Both Boards felt this could be one way to say "thank you" to Saint Meinrad for the educational opportunities Saint Meinrad has provided.

Details of the renovation are included in the enclosed brochure. I ask you to take part in this endeavor. Join in this Alumni effort by sending in your gift today. With your help, we Alumni of Saint Meinrad will make the refurbishing of the Archabbey Church towers, clocks, and bells a reality.

Sincerely yours,

C. Allen Boedeker
Summer Session Alumni President

Saint Meinrad Archabbey

ST. MEINRAD, IN 47577

812: 357-6611

OFFICE OF THE ARCHABBOT

May 15, 1995

Dear _____ ,

My days in the office of Archabbot of Saint Meinrad are coming to a close. This has been a time to pause and reflect on the last seventeen years . . . a period both rewarding and challenging for me, personally, and for the Saint Meinrad community.

One of the most rewarding aspects of my tenure as Archabbot has been the opportunity to witness the commitment and partnership of people of faith—people like you who assist us with our work.

I want to take this opportunity to thank you again for your recent gift of support for the operations of our Schools. This support is vital to the continuing work of Saint Meinrad. I also want to extend to you, now, the opportunity to join with us in a very special project . . . the renewal of the heart of Saint Meinrad—the Archabbey Church. This project was begun nearly 25 years ago but was never fully completed.

The renovation will accomplish a number of goals. The mechanical systems of the church will be updated. A new Blessed Sacrament Chapel and Shrine of Our Lady of Einsiedeln will be located within the church. Perhaps most importantly, the current floor plan of two levels will be altered so that the entire church will be on one level. This will benefit our physically challenged monks and visitors.

The enclosed brochure gives more details on the project. We are ready, now, to begin the work of renewing this historic church, which is at the center of all we do here at Saint Meinrad.

I ask you to renew your partnership with Saint Meinrad by investing in this endeavor. Together, we can ensure that the Archabbey Church will continue to symbolize the partnership Saint Meinrad continues to enjoy with its many generous friends.

Gratefully yours in Christ,

Timothy, OSB

Rt. Rev. Timothy Sweeney, OSB
Archabbot

Commemorative Opportunities

In accomplishing the renovation of Archabbey Church, there will be several opportunities to memorialize loved ones. Commemorative opportunities in the renewal of Saint Meinrad's House of the Lord are a fitting way to honor beloved family members, friends, or monks, and to express gratitude to God for abundant blessings.

Donors of gifts of $25,000 or more will be appropriately recognized in the renovated church or the plaza outside the main entrance to the Church. In addition, all who contribute to the renovation project will be listed in a Book of Benefactors to be displayed in a place of honor within the Church.

If you are interested in commemorating a loved one, a former teacher, or an esteemed monk in the renewal of the Archabbey Church, please contact:

Mr. Daniel A. Schipp
Vice President for
    Development
Saint Meinrad Archabbey
St. Meinrad, IN 47577
(800) 682-0988

Renewing the Heart of Saint Meinrad

$\mathcal{T}$he Archabbey Church of Our Lady of Einsiedeln is a very special place to the monks, alumni and students at Saint Meinrad. More than an outstanding example of Romanesque architecture, a beloved building, and the place where the monks mark the stages of their monastic life and students celebrate important events during their passage through the Schools, the Archabbey Church is the life-giving heart and spiritual center of Saint Meinrad. For nearly ninety years, the bells of the Archabbey Church have called monks, students, and guests to daily tasks and to an awareness of God's presence in their lives.

The Archabbey Church itself stands as a symbol of the partnership between Saint Meinrad and its friends. Just as the monks and people from the area worked side-by-side to build the church, so now Saint Meinrad works hand-in-hand with Alumni and friends in carrying on its mission.

An initial renovation on the Archabbey Church began over twenty-five years ago. At the completion of the first phase of that project, the monks paused to reflect on how best to proceed with the second phase. As the demands of the Schools and other needs intruded, this period of reflection stretched until just recently. More than a year ago, Archabbot Timothy Sweeney appointed a committee of monks to coordinate the development of theological and liturgical principles to guide a resumed renovation.

Elements of the Renovation

The floor plan will respect the original architectural concept of the church while eliminating the two levels. Having the church on one level provides greater flexibility, ease of celebration, and better access for the elderly and physically challenged. The altar, the focal point of the church, will remain near the west entrance.

The upper level of the church will be lowered and the transept galleries removed. Wooden choir stalls will be placed in the transept for the monastic community. Guests will be situated west of the choir stalls.

A new Blessed Sacrament Chapel within the Archabbey Church will form an integral part of the overall design. This chapel will be larger than the present temporary chapel and will probably include at least part of the old gold altar that had been in the apse of the Archabbey Church prior to the 1960s renovation.

The painted glass windows will be preserved, repaired and cleaned. Natural and artificial light are important to the overall scheme of the renovated Archabbey Church.

A shrine honoring Our Lady of Einsiedeln, the patroness of the Archabbey Church, will be erected in a place of prominence within the church. Here will stand the cherished statue of Our Lady of Einsiedeln.

The massive pipe organ, rebuilt in the early 1960s from the original Estey organ, will remain the primary musical instrument in the church. The pipeworks currently in the north gallery will probably be relocated.

The current flooring will be replaced with beautiful and durable stone.

The furnishings will strive to reflect the monastic values and practices of authenticity, simplicity, stability and craftsmanship.

Mechanical systems will be upgraded. The renovation plans include new electrical, lighting, sound, heating and air-conditioning systems.

Structural improvements are needed to keep the church in excellent condition. Drainage will be improved, the exterior stone will be tuck-pointed and the roof insulated. In addition, the gold crosses and *fleurs-de-lis* will be regilded.

In the Archabbey Church towers, the clocks will be repaired and Bell Number Six, which cracked in 1973, will be recast or replaced.

A plaza will be built immediately outside the west, or main, entrance to the church. Once the renovation is complete, guests will be encouraged to enter the church through the west doors.

This plan lays out a direction in which the renovation work will develop. The details of the plan remain to be worked out.

☩ ☩ ☩ ☩ ☩ ☩ ☩ ☩

A Most Worthwhile Endeavor

Because the Archabbey Church plays such a central role in the life of Saint Meinrad, the decision to move forward with its renovation has been made only after much prayer, reflection and consultation. The projected cost of $4.5 million is a large investment, but we believe it must be weighed in light of the impact it will have on the monks, students, alumni, and guests who will be drawn closer to God by their prayer in the Archabbey Church. It must also consider what the church symbolizes about Saint Meinrad and witnesses to the world: God's constant presence in our lives, the centrality of prayer, and the treasured tradition of monks and benefactors joined together in prayer and work.

Asking God's blessing on the work of renovating the Archabbey Church, the monks of Saint Meinrad invite you to participate generously in this most worthwhile endeavor. They pray that in this renewal of Saint Meinrad's nearly century-old House of the Lord, as in all things, *God may be glorified.*

> **One thing I asked of the Lord,**
> **that will I seek after;**
> **to live in the house of the Lord**
> **all the days of my life,**
> **to behold the beauty of the Lord**
> **and to inquire in his temple.**
>
> Ps. 27:4

We Invite Your Partnership

The renovation of the Archabbey Church involves more than just the renewal of a building. It also embraces the renewal of individuals, a community, and an institution. Saint Meinrad's Archabbey Church symbolizes, in a physical and enduring way, faith in God's abiding presence in individual lives; a community's devotion to its prayer and worship; and an institution's confidence in and commitment to the future.

You are invited to join other friends of Saint Meinrad who have already committed their financial support to renewing the "Heart of Saint Meinrad." For this renewal to become a reality, Saint Meinrad needs your help.

The projected cost of the renovation is $4.5 million. Already $4 million has been pledged toward the project. Although the cost of the renovation is substantial, little has been spent on the Archabbey Church since it was finished in 1907. Even the 1968 renovation was accomplished at minimal expense. For all practical purposes, the heating, electrical and lighting systems in the church have not been updated in 90 years.

The meaning and the motivation for everything Saint Meinrad is and does flows from the Archabbey Church. Your partnership is vital in accomplishing this renovation. The Saint Meinrad community invites you to generously participate in this most worthwhile endeavor.

Objectives of the Renovation of Archabbey Church

By undertaking this renovation, Saint Meinrad, with the help of alumni and friends, will be:

Enhancing the celebration of liturgy at Saint Meinrad for monks, students and guests alike.

Praising God by renewing His holy temple.

Preserving a sacred space which is

☨ the very heart of Saint Meinrad, the place where the very meaning of monastic life is experienced and expressed;

☨ the center of Saint Meinrad, the focal point for the entire Archabbey community—monks, students, co-workers, alumni, and friends;

☨ a defining element of Saint Meinrad, symbolizing the institution's rock-solid foundation, its tradition of partnership with neighbors and benefactors, and its aspirations, confidence and faith; and

☨ a local landmark, an impressive example of Romanesque art and architecture, which represents Saint Meinrad's stability and service to the community.

Saint Meinrad Archabbey
St. Meinrad, IN 47577

Press Release Announcing a Large Gift by an Individual

Press Release

For Immediate Release

Date: December 14, 2000
Contact: Maia S. Kingman
          Publications
Phone: 219-866-6418

Million Dollar Donor Says Saint Joseph's College Graduates are "Proven Products"

Rensselaer—John Boler, founder and chairman of The Boler Company, visited the Saint Joseph's College campus Wednesday to deliver a $1 million check to College President Albert J. Shannon. "I had pledged $1 million to the College over four years," he said, "but I know that small colleges are often in need of money, so I brought the whole thing today," he announced, smiling.

Boler explained to a group of Saint Joseph's faculty, students, and administrators, that he has a firm belief in the value of a private, Catholic education. Having experienced personalized care at John Carroll, a small Jesuit University in Cleveland, Ohio, he sent his children to Catholic colleges as well. His son, James, is a 1985 graduate of Saint Joseph's College. "I see the values that a Catholic education has instilled in my children," he said. "My children are good citizens; they are participants in their own families; they understand the privilege of giving back to their communities."

"The faculty here are to be commended," he said. "You have many fine alumni to be proud of. A Saint Joseph's College graduate is a proven product." For Catholic colleges like Saint Joseph's to continue to be able to create a student who is "over and above" other students, Boler said, they need financial support. "I hope the money I bring you today encourages other friends of the College to give."

In that spirit, the Boler donation has been used to issue The Boler Challenge for Academic Excellence, a dollar-for-dollar matching program. The Boler Challenge encourages friends of the College to support academic initiatives, including faculty development, international programs, service learning programs, new course development, and teaching equipment. Renovation projects that the Boler Challenge will facilitate include laboratories and classrooms located in the Arts and Sciences building.

When asked about the significance of a $1 million donation, President Shannon said that it makes a "tremendous impact" on a college the size of Saint Joseph's. "There is no doubt that it will change lives here. Whether through a new chemistry lab, new classroom equipment, or new classes, students' lives will be directly impacted." David Chattin, Vice President for Academic Affairs, says that Boler's gift will allow the College "to do things we were only able to dream of" before.

Boler's donation is one of three $1 million gifts made in the College's history. The others were made by James P. and Susan Lennane, for whom the College's Computer Center is named, and Peter Shen, for whom the Banet Core Education Center's large auditorium is named. These three $1 million gifts are the largest donations in the College's history, and with his history of giving to Saint Joseph's College, Boler has become the College's largest single donor.

Boler is founder and chairman of The Boler Company, which is among the largest privately held vendors to the transportation industry. The Boler Company is the parent company of Hendrickson International, one of the world's leading manufacturers of suspension systems and components for heavy-duty trucks and trailers. Hendrickson is a major supplier to every North American heavy-duty truck and trailer manufacturer, as well as many manufacturers in Europe, Australia, Mexico, Japan, and Latin America.

Of his success in business, Boler says that his Catholic education taught him to have a "deep commitment to sharing my accomplishments." In presenting the check to President Shannon, he said he hoped the College would not only match the money in the Boler Challenge, but "better it many times over."

Appeal Letter to Donor Recognition Group

The Fellows of Saint Joseph's College

P.O. Box 870
Rensselaer, IN 47978
(219) 866-6250
(800) 227-1898

The 109th Year of the College
*Jubilee — A Year of Praise
and Thanksgiving* — John Paul II

March 2000

Dear College Fellow:

Since their installation in 1910–11, the magnificent stained glass windows of Saint Joseph's Chapel have been a spiritual and artistic treasure of the College, influencing the lives of thousands of Saint Joseph's College students. Perhaps you may remember seeing them for the first time as a young student, or as a visitor to campus.

The windows are unique in depicting stories that relate to the education of young adults. One window shows Jesus as a young boy before the learned teachers and scribes in the temple. Another depicts Saint John Berchmas, the patron saint of youth. And a third shows Saint Catherine of Alexandria, a patroness of philosophers, who represents wisdom, education and loyalty. In all, there are 20 stained glass windows, 12 of which adorn the interior of the sanctuary.

Unfortunately time and weather have taken their toll on the leading and steel structures that hold the windows in place. Several windows are severely bowed, and one was blown out by severe weather in the winter of 1998.

Last year, the Council of Fellows took on the challenge of raising the funds to fully restore the windows of Saint Joseph's Chapel and preserve them for generations to come. We knew it would not be an easy task, *but we also knew that, when asked, you and other Fellows of Saint Joseph's College would respond generously.*

And so far you have.

In the past 10 months about 45 percent of the $200,000 goal has been pledged by the Fellows of Saint Joseph's College. Reconstruction work began on February 2nd.

But, we are not finished yet. Work on the windows can be undertaken only as gifts are received. We must continue to move forward, *asking each Fellow to make a special, sacrificial contribution over and above all else that you do for Saint Joseph's College, to help restore the windows.* The sooner we reach the goal, the sooner work on the windows can be completed.

The restoration of this historical treasure is dependent upon many gifts from College Fellows to achieve the $200,000 goal. Because you are a current Fellow of Saint Joseph's

College, *you have the very special privilege of sponsoring a new Fellow with your gift of $2,000 or more* toward the windows restoration project. Think of what it might mean to sponsor a family member, friend, or colleague while helping restore the stained glass windows of Saint Joseph's Chapel to their original magnificence.

If the current economy has blessed you and your family, please consider underwriting the renovation of a single window. A gift of appreciated securities from your portfolio, or a paid-up life insurance policy that is no longer needed for its original purpose, may be an ideal way for you to make your gift. A metal plaque will be installed beneath each sponsored window to recognize your gift or to honor a family member or loved one you designate. Several members of your family may wish to join together in sponsoring a window through a family gift. Yet, regardless of the amount you give, please know that it will be gratefully received and wisely used.

The enclosed brochure contains additional important information, listing all the opportunities for giving. Please read it carefully, and, if you have any questions at all, feel free to call me at (219) 866-6205. It would be my privilege to speak with you about this important project.

Your gift is terribly important and critical to our success. Please use the enclosed form to make *your pledge of support before May 15th* so that I may list you as a contributor in the annual Fellows Dinner program this year. If you can, please use your gift to sponsor a new Fellow—a privilege available only to current Fellows.

Thank you. With God's Blessing, I know that you will do all that you can.

Sincerely,

[signature]

John B. Egan, Ph.D.
Chairman, Council of Fellows

P.S. What a pleasure it will be to list your name as a contributor in the program for the annual Fellows Dinner on Saturday, June 3rd! But, to do so, I must have your pledge of support by May 15th. Please don't delay. Your gift is critical to the restoration of the windows of Saint Joseph's Chapel.

The Fellows of Saint Joseph's College

July 1999

Dear Fellow:

The annual Fellows Dinner held on June 5th was one of the best attended in many years. Over 250 Fellows and their guests shared in the entertainment, fellowship and delightful menu. I was pleased to serve as master of ceremonies and look forward to the same task next year. At the dinner we inducted 31 new Fellows into our ranks.

But, aside from a report on the dinner, this letter is about some exciting new developments in the Fellows Program. For several weeks this past spring I was privileged to meet with a group of College Fellows to consider how the Fellows Program could be strengthened and enhanced for the future. Many ideas were proposed and discussed. Some were discarded, others revised and adopted. Our guiding principle in considering change was always that current Fellows would continue to be accorded the recognition and privileges to which they have always been entitled. Any changes would affect only new Fellows inducted after July 1, 1999.

The enclosed brochure, *A Time for Renewal,* outlines the changes we adopted for the Fellows Program. The initial gift for new Fellows has been increased to $2,000; and, as important, current and new Fellows will be recognized for cumulative lifetime giving. I know you will be as excited as I am about the positive effect these changes will have on the future of the program.

Equally significant is the establishment of the *Council of Fellows.* The purpose of the Council is to advise the President of the College and to oversee the growth of the Fellows Program.

But truly the most exciting activity in my mind for Fellows since the program was established by Father Gross in 1962, is the commitment we have made to raise the funds to restore the magnificent stained glass windows of Saint Joseph's Chapel to their original splendor and glory.

The Chapel windows were created by Francis Xavier Zettler of Munich, Germany, and installed in 1912, a year after the Chapel was dedicated. Over the years, leading that holds stained glass windows together corrodes and must be replaced every 100 years or so. Each window in the Chapel will cost $25,000 to renew, and it will take a year to fully restore the windows.

Kenneth J. Ahler, M.D., '63, has graciously accepted the mantle of leadership for this project. Later this year you will be hearing directly from him, asking for your special gift for the Chapel windows. Gifts of many sizes will be needed, from $1,000 to $30,000 and more, to reach the $250,000 goal, and every Fellow will be asked to make a special gift over and above your ongoing contribution to the College. Each gift of $2,000 to the Chapel window project may also be used to sponsor a new Fellow. When our task is complete a plaque recognizing all who contributed will be permanently mounted in the Chapel. Restoration of the windows will begin as soon as the first $25,000 is raised.

Once completed, the renewal of the windows will be a lasting and wonderful tribute to the very special role that Fellows play at Saint Joseph's College. The newly restored windows will again be a true College and Rensselaer treasure that will inspire and uplift generations of friends, alumni and their families when they visit the Chapel.

The future of Saint Joseph's College is very bright. I am honored to be the first chairman of the Council of Fellows. Please mark your calendar now for Saturday, June 3, 2000, to join me at the annual Fellows Dinner. I look forward to seeing you.

Sincerely yours,

John B. Egan, Ph.D.
Chairman, Council of Fellows

P.S. I have enclosed a Fellows Sponsorship/Nomination form for you to sponsor a new Fellow this year. Your gift, unless you specify otherwise, will go toward the Chapel window renewal program.

*The Fellows of
Saint Joseph's College*

*A Time for

Renewal*

*The dawn of a new century is an opportunity
to examine the past, to reconsider the present
and to look confidently toward the future.
It is a time of reinvigoration and renewal.*

June 5, 1999

ESIGNATION AS A FELLOW is one of the highest non-academic honors that can be bestowed by Saint Joseph's College. Originally, in the seventeenth century a Fellow was either a member of the governing board of Oxford University or a duke or earl who represented the university in his part of England. In addition, the Fellow was a counselor, patron and benefactor as manifested by gifts of land, buildings and money. Since 1664, the title of Fellow has also been the mark of outstanding and privileged membership in professional and academic associations. It is an honor granted only to persons who have made significant contributions personally, professionally and financially. Indeed, the first and primary meaning of the term "fellow" is "one who lays down money in a joint undertaking with others." A Saint Joseph's College Fellow "is one who sees beyond the horizons of his daily routine and particular profession to a personal identification with the College, its prestige and its mission." Accepting the mantle of Fellow means that an individual accepts a solemn lifetime obligation to support Saint Joseph's College with his or her work, wisdom and wealth.

HEN THE SAINT JOSEPH'S COLLEGE FELLOWS PROGRAM was established by Father Gross in 1962 the $1,000 Fellows contribution was an especially large gift for even the most generous of donors. Today, 37 years later, the $1,000 minimum contribution (payable over three years) remains unchanged. Were it to reflect inflation, the amount would be $5,500. And were it to reflect its value in relation to tuition, room and board, it would be more than $10,000. Without renewal the distinction of being a Fellow is in danger of becoming a hollow honor.

I N THE SPIRIT OF RENEWAL, on March 10, 1999, President Albert Shannon assembled a group of Saint Joseph's College Fellows to examine the past, present and future of the Fellows Program to assure that it remains a vital force for Saint Joseph's College well into the next century. Over a six-week period the *ad hoc* Fellows committee met several times to consider how the Fellows Program could be renewed. Many ideas, some conflicting, were thoughtfully discussed and debated. Throughout the debate, the guiding principle was *every current Fellow will continue to be recognized and accorded all the rights and privileges to which he or she has been entitled in the past.* The College has made a solemn commitment to the Fellows and will honor that commitment. At its final meeting on May 25th the committee endorsed enhancements to the Fellows Program *effective on July 1, 1999 for newly inducted Fellows.*

To sponsor or become a new Fellow after July 1, 1999, will require a gift of $2,000. To encourage continued growth of the Fellows Program, the minimum gift to become a new Fellow will be $2,000 effective July 1, 1999. The gift may be paid by a pledge of $400 per year for five years by either the new Fellow or Sponsor.

Fellows will be honored for their cumulative lifetime support of the College. As all current and new Fellows achieve higher levels of cumulative lifetime giving to the College, they will be recognized at the annual Fellows Dinner for their extraordinary support in one of the categories below.

Designation	Cumulative Lifetime Giving
Saint Gaspar Fellow	$1,000,000
Halas Fellow	$500,000
Halleck Fellow	$250,000
McHale Fellow	$100,000
Presidential Fellow	$50,000
Father Gross Fellow	$25,000
Father Bierberg Fellow	$5,000
New Fellow	$2,000
Fellow (current)	$1,000

A Council of Fellows will advise and assist the College. A *Council of Fellows* will be appointed by the President to oversee the Fellows Program, to receive nominations and confirm new Fellows, to advise the President on the Fellows Program and to actively participate in developing increased financial support for the College.

Fellows shall be asked to contribute on an annual basis. Every Fellow shall be encouraged to make an annual contribution to Saint Joseph's College of at least $200 to take advantage of the Indiana tax credit for contributions to colleges. The Council of Fellows will select an appropriate project and goal to which Fellows will be encouraged to contribute. New Fellows who contribute each year will receive an invitation to the Fellows Dinner. If a Fellow does not contribute at any level for a period of three years, he or she may be designated *inactive* by the Council of Fellows.

The annual Fellows Dinner will be enhanced to become once again the premier,

non-academic event on campus. The annual Fellows Dinner held each year on the first Saturday of June will be returned to the level of graciousness and significance it initially had. It will become once again the premier, non-academic event sponsored by the College, rivaling the annual Trustee Scholarship Dinner. *Active Fellows and their spouses will be invited to attend as guests of Saint Joseph's College. Additional tickets for guests of individual Fellows will be priced to reflect the increased cost of the dinner.*

Fellows who have rendered extraordinary service to the College may be honored by their peers. The Council of Fellows may recommend to the President from time to time that certain Fellows who have distinguished themselves over a lifetime of giving to Saint Joseph's College be designated as *Distinguished Fellows* and *Life Fellows.*

Benefits and honors accorded to Fellows will be enhanced. In addition to the Fellows certificate and the privilege of wearing the Fellows rosette, Fellows will receive an annual privilege card that will confer specific benefits while on campus. These benefits may include admission to all athletic events on campus without charge; admission and special receptions at cultural/arts programs on campus; admission to Lake Banet Park without charge; circulation privileges at the Robinson Memorial Library; use of the Board of Trustees room for private functions and a monthly copy of the *President's Newsletter.*

**Ad Hoc Committee on the Future
of the Fellows Program**

Fellows from the Community
Kenneth J. Ahler, M.D., '63
John R. Baumann, '61
Thomas J. Effinger, '65
Larry Jenkins
R. Gordon Klockow, D.D.S.
Honorable J. Philip McGraw, '70
Edson W. Murray
Donald P. Steiner
George J. Tonner, '43
Michael J. Vallone, '60
Carol J. Wood, '74

Fellows from the College
Albert J. Shannon, Ph.D.
Anne-Marie Egan
John B. Egan, Ph.D.
Maureen V. Egan, '90
Cindy Foster
John Milentis

SAINT JOSEPH'S COLLEGE
INDIANA

The Fellows Program
Rensselaer, IN 47978
(219) 866-6250
(800) 227-1898

Saint Joseph's College
1999 - 2000

HONOR ROLL OF DONORS

SAINT JOSEPH'S COLLEGE

The Honor Roll of Donors
1999–2000

Welcome

Highlights of 1999–2000

Top Ten Giving Classes

President's Circle

Father Charles Banet Club

Twin Towers Club

Parents

Friends

Alumni Giving by Class Year

Corporations, Foundations and Organizations

Heritage Scroll of Honor

Donors to Chapel Windows Project

Bequests and Estate Gifts

Cover Photo: Saint Joseph's Chapel, dedicated May 17, 1910. Indiana Governor Thomas R. Marshall delivered the 1910 congratulatory speech whose theme was "Indiana school that educates both heart and head." Ninety years later, that theme remains the cornerstone of our College mission.

This photo of the Chapel was taken prior to 1965. The summer of 1965 brought with it changes that were made in the Chapel, reflecting the liturgical reforms of Vatican Council II. Altars were removed from the sanctuary, while the altars in the nave and the communion rail had been previously removed. The "renovation" would not be complete until March 1976.

Summer 2000

In the 1999–2000 Honor Roll of Donors you will see the 3,811 alumni, parents, friends and organizations that supported the mission of Saint Joseph's College. It is only because of these people that SJC is able to deliver the margin of excellence that we have for going on one hundred and eleven years.

It is with a great feeling of pride that we provide you with these names. These are the people who have chosen to support the mission of SJC financially and for that we are very appreciative.

This year's Honor Roll of Donors is different than in years past. In an effort to be the best stewards of your contributions, we have been frugal with extra expenses. It is our belief that you would rather have your contributions and gifts go toward enriching student's lives directly than on "extras."

So once again, thank you. We shall continue to work diligently to earn your continuing interest, pride and commitment.

Albert J. Shannon, Ph.D.
President

K. P. McClanahan
Vice President for Institutional Advancement

Maureen 'Mo' Egan '90
Assistant Vice President, Major and Planned Giving

Steven P. Brady
College Fund Manager

James Wirtes '97
Alumni and Parents Relations Manager

1999–2000 Year in Review

◆ Saint Joseph's College saw the largest entering freshman class in the past fifteen years. Enrollment this fall was 934.

◆ This summer a new $3.3 million, 95-student residential suite apartment complex was opened. It is the first new student residence since Justin Hall was completed in 1968.

◆ The Templeton Foundation recently recognized Saint Joseph's College as a leader in the development of student character. Arthur J. Schwartz, Ed.D., of the Temple Foundation said, *"Saint Joseph's College has a strong commitment to character development, and the strength of its program makes it a model for colleges and universities nationwide. Saint Joseph's work in this area is most impressive."*

◆ The Class of 1960 donated a new competition 6-lane track and field. This will allow the nationally ranked track team to start holding NCAA competitions at Saint Joseph's College this fall.

◆ The Board of Trustees looked toward the future and accepted a new Master Facilities Plan, which will keep Saint Joseph's competitive with other colleges and universities. This is a $72 million plan that will be completed in the next twenty years.

◆ The Fellows have had an incredibly successful year. Sixty-five new Fellows were inducted this spring in a special ceremony in Saint Joseph's Chapel. The Fellows also have surpassed their original goal of $200,000 for the renovation and restoration of the Chapel windows by $100,000! Restoration of the Chapel windows will be completed by the next Fellows Dinner in June 2001.

◆ The Teacher Education program received high marks in the continuing accreditation by the National Council for the Accreditation of Teachers Education (NCATE) this spring. This reflects the high standards in the Teacher Education program that Saint Joseph's College has set.

Saint Joseph's College Donors

Top Ten Giving Classes by Gift Amount

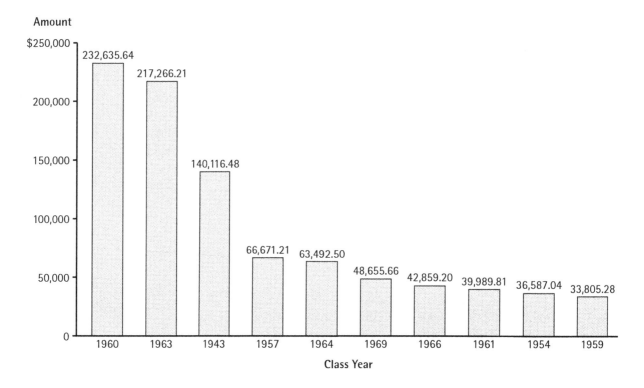

Top Ten Giving Classes by Participation

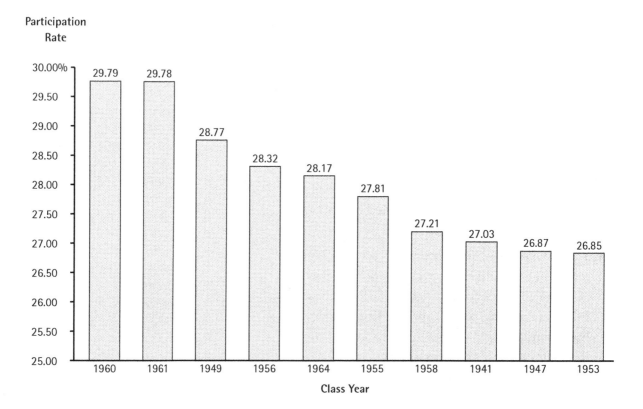

Saint Joseph's College Donors

A Record of Giving to Saint Joseph's College

[Giving categories and total gift amounts are shown. Names of donors have been omitted to protect donors' privacy. The differences in amounts between the figures and this list are due to differences in the time covered.]

President's Circle, $10,000.00 and up

Father Charles Banet Club, $5,000.00–$9,999.99

Twin Towers Club, $1,000.00–$4,999.99

Parents

Friends

Class Giving

Class of 1929, $50.00

Class of 1930, $100.00

Class of 1931, $100.00

Class of 1932, $1,340.00

Class of 1933, $2,100.00

Class of 1934, $160.00

Class of 1935. $1,625.00

Class of 1936, $1,010.00

Class of 1937, $350.00

Class of 1938, $4,875.00

Class of 1939, $1,325.00

Class of 1940, $6,272.70

Class of 1941, $17,310.88

Class of 1942, $3,183.00

Class of 1943, $136,016.48

Class of 1944, $750.00

Class of 1945, $5,105.00

Class of 1946, $505.00

Class of 1947, $5,193.56

Class of 1948, $2,500.00

Class of 1949, $6,705.00

Class of 1950, $19,342.75

Class of 1951, $28,435.00

Class of 1952, $8,244.25

Class of 1953, $4,745.00

Class of 1954, $33,457.36

Class of 1955, $5,865.00

Class of 1956, $11,140.00

Class of 1957, $59,756.21

Class of 1958, $4,405.00

Class of 1959, $21,132.00

Class of 1960, $158,732.12

Class of 1961, $34,431.41

Class of 1962, $25,990.20

Class of 1963, $190,396.21

Class of 1964, $56,287.50

Class of 1965, $19,554.47

Class of 1966, $23,249.20

Class of 1967, $9,800.00

Class of 1968, $14,083.84

Class of 1969, $34,905.58

Class of 1970, $9,249.00

Class of 1971, $12,128.56

Class of 1972, $6,350.00

Class of 1973, $9,808.96

Class of 1974, $11,620.00

Class of 1975, $19,815.25

Class of 1976, $5,237.00

Class of 1977, $6,997.50

Class of 1978, $5,315.00

Class of 1979, $14,090.00

Class of 1980, $20,296.90

Class of 1981, $2,735.00

Class of 1982, $1,385.00

Class of 1983, $2,855.00

Class of 1984, $4,780.00

Class of 1985, $1,540.00

Class of 1986, $4,180.00

Class of 1987, $6,165.00

Class of 1988, $1,905.00

Class of 1989, $1,225.00
Class of 1990, $4,510.00
Class of 1991, $1,456.00
Class of 1992, $625.00
Class of 1993, $1,095.00
Class of 1994, $510.00
Class of 1995, $585.00
Class of 1996, $310.00
Class of 1997, $760.00
Class of 1998, $470.00
Class of 1999, $30.00

**Corporations, Foundations
and Organizations**

Heritage Scroll of Honor
In grateful recognition of those individuals
who have made provisions for SJC in their
estate plans.

*This listing is a reflection of our current records.
To report an omission or error please call the
number listed below. For further information or
to learn how you can become a part of the Heritage Scroll of Honor contact Maureen Egan '90
at (219) 866-6250*

**Donors to Saint Joseph's Chapel Windows
Project**

Bequests and Estate Gifts

Lightning Source UK Ltd.
Milton Keynes UK
UKOW07f0653231217
314976UK00001B/10/P